Growing Together in Marriage

Growing Together in Marriage

J. Murray Elwood

AVE MARIA PRESS / NOTRE DAME / INDIANA 46556

Library of Congress Catalog Card Number: 76-51468
International Standard Book Number: 0-87793-128-3

© 1977 by Ave Maria Press, Notre Dame, Indiana
  All rights reserved.

Photography: H. Armstrong Roberts, cover, 2, 8, 14, 28, 56,
              74, 120, 148, 164; Robert Maust, 8;
              Jim Whitmer, 42, 102; Sylvia Brownell, 112;
              J. Murray Elwood, 94, 134;
              Sunrise Photos, 175.

Printed in the United States of America

For Melanie and Michael

While still I may, I write for you
The love I lived, the dream I knew.
— William Butler Yeats

Contents

Preface / 9

Introduction by Joseph M. Champlin / 11

1   Can This Marriage Be Saved? / 15

2   Impossible Dreams / 29

3   Silent Words, Unspoken Feelings / 43

4   On the Dotted Line . . . / 57

5   Is Our Marriage O.K.? / 75

6   Free To Be You and Me! / 95

7   Two's a Couple, Three's a Crowd? / 113

8   What Is This Thing Called Love? / 135

9   Love Grows with Loving / 149

10   Friends and Lovers / 165

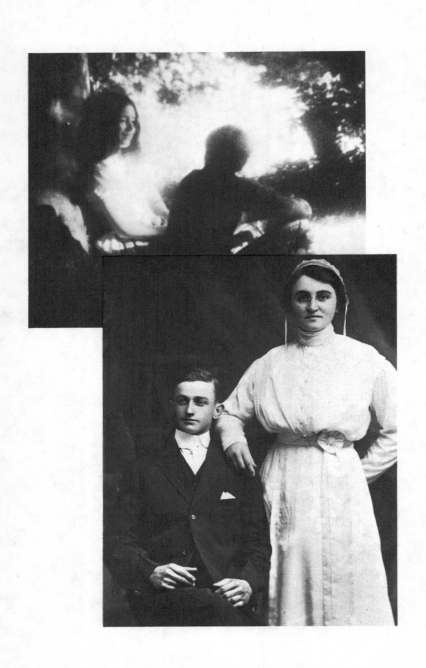

Preface

Thomas Merton, that great writer, observed once that the poetry of Dylan Thomas made him feel ashamed. It was depressing, commented Merton, that those who say they love God write so poorly, while those who do not believe in him take pains to write so well. It wasn't just grammar and syntax, Merton added, but having something to say and saying it in sentences that were not half dead.

Growing Together in Marriage was written because I believe that faith—a religious perspective—offers many rich insights into the meaning of life and love and marriage. Religious writing about marriage, however, seems sometimes so theologically dense or unrealistically romantic that one wonders about its appeal. There are those couples, I am sure, who are genuinely interested in marriage as ministry or as a sign of the Covenant, but *Growing Together in Marriage* is written for men and women whose concerns are more "mundane"—for those who seek richer lives and more deeply satisfying marriages.

So this book is for couples already married, or for

those thinking about marriage, who are much more comfortable reading the pages of a best-seller or a popular magazine than they are with a religious article or a Catholic book. It has always seemed reasonable to me that if a psychology of human behavior or a new personality theory can be interestingly presented to a general audience (as, for example, in Gail Sheehy's *Passages*) by good writing and a creative style, then it should also be possible to describe a theology of marriage in an equally attractive way, with words not "half dead."

Growing Together in Marriage is about the lives and loves of real people—Andrea and Brian, Greg and Carol, Wanda and Ralph, David and Laurie, Ray and Janet. It is also due to the help and friendship of many other generous people. To them, especially, I would like to express my gratitude: to Paul Briand, a truly creative writer, who so unselfishly took time from his busy class schedule and preparation of his own new book, to read the manuscript in its entirety, polish its style and offer much enthusiastic encouragement and support; to Sylvia Brownell who helped with the dialogue and characterization and made the rough words smooth; to Dick Blaise, Bob Elwood, Mary Hurlburt, William Kehoe, Edward O'Heron, John Readling and Jack Ziegler for their insights, suggestions and assistance at various stages of preparation; to Gene Geissler and Charles Jones for their editorial advice; and, lastly, I owe a very special word of thanks to my secretary, Loraine Juchniewicz, who was not only the first to suggest this book, but whose creative talents and professional skills so carefully prepared it for publication.

Introduction

by Joseph M. Champlin

Father J. Murray Elwood is an inspiring speaker, a sensitive clergy-counselor and an avid student of contemporary society. For over 20 years he has used and developed those skills and interests in a variety of ways with young people—as a parish priest, as the principal of a Catholic high school and, since 1966, as campus minister for students at the State University of New York in Oswego.

That background and those qualities come across in this, Father Elwood's first book. *Growing Together in Marriage* takes a thorough look at an age-old institution suffering in our day either open attack or severe stress. The text studies this topic through numerous miniature case studies, the best-known findings of contemporary psychology and illustrations from modern literature.

The case studies are interesting and relatable, some even quite inspiring. His popularization of psychology today makes Dr. Eric Berne, Dr. Thomas Harris et al., more easily understandable. Father Elwood's excerpts from current novels, magazines and musical favorites accentuate the here-and-now approach of the book.

The author doesn't duck tough questions. Having worked closely with college-age persons over the past 10 years, he knows the sharp issues which confront them: childless-by-choice marriages, couples living together, group sex, women's liberation, shifting roles for modern men, personal fulfillment. He offers here insights, not simple solutions. The insights, though expressed in the language of the present, are based on traditional values.

Growing Together in Marriage seeks, as its main thrust, to clarify the concept of love in the modern world and in contemporary marriages. It argues that love, properly understood, has the power to save marriages and the institution of marriage. It also maintains that such love is the true source of real growth both for individuals and couples.

I recommend this text for all serious students of marriage in the modern world, for young people preparing to enter a marital union and for those husbands and wives who care about their relationship and wish to see that bond grow.

Chapter 1
Can This Marriage Be Saved?

When Andrea and Brian were married 12 years ago, those of us who were present for their wedding felt that, if ever a marriage was made in heaven, this was it. At 23 and a Catholic college graduate, Andrea was one of those radiantly beautiful brides seen only on the pages of *Vogue* or *Mademoiselle.* She had worked in the business world for a couple of years after graduation; she was bright, attractive and mature. Then she met Brian who, as she described him, was different from any man she had ever dated. Brian *was* different in those days. At 25, he looked as if he could still play end for Notre Dame. Just out of Harvard Law, Brian knew what he wanted in life. And that included Andrea, a family, and a future.

So they walked down the aisle and out of the church, two happy, mature people who were now one. They had been promised, through the liturgy, that although life was always a mixture of joy and sorrow, laughter and tears, they could expect from their marriage "the fullest measure of happiness allotted to man in this vale of tears."

But after 12 years of marriage and three children, all this has changed. The bright promise of tomorrow has become, for this couple, a world painted grey with frustration and failure. There used to be so much to share, so many things to say. Now, they talk only to argue about the children and the condition of the house. Brian complains about Andrea's housekeeping or that she lets the kids get away with murder. Andrea responds with her own pet peeves—her slim weekly allowance, Brian's late hours of work; the children don't even know their own father!

The only thing this couple seems to have in common is that they know each other's vulnerabilities. Brian hasn't advanced in his firm as quickly as some other young lawyers. Some days he feels worthless and a failure. Andrea blames his lack of initiative. "He was spoiled rotten by his mother and sisters," she says. "They waited on him hand and foot."

On the other hand, Andrea *is* only an average housekeeper, as Brian knows. "We live in a dump," he complains, "because she's on the phone all day long with her girl friends." Andrea feels used, because she is the one who has made all the sacrifices while Brian takes a couple of afternoons off each week to play golf with his friends. There are arguments, yes, but now only a frightening, cold indifference hardens between Brian and Andrea. Once they had wondered how they could ever live *without* each other, now they both seriously question whether they can go on living *with* each other.

Brian drinks too much, works late too many nights at the office, and admits, privately, that he enjoys the after-hours company of one of his secretaries rather than go home and face Andrea and the three children. But, when asked, he says he still loves Andrea.

Andrea has now begun taking graduate courses at a nearby university. She talks, these days, more and more of a career after marriage and uses language borrowed from the women's movement, words like "identity," and "self-fulfillment." Recently, she bought new clothes, changed her hair style and, after evening class, has started visiting a singles' bar with a divorced girl friend to talk and dance and, as she says, "to have a little fun." Does she still love Brian? Andrea isn't sure.

WHAT'S HAPPENING TO MARRIAGE?

The real question about Brian and Andrea is not so much can their marriage be saved, but can *marriage* itself survive. What is happening to marriage? Where are the dreams of yesteryear? Not only is it the torrent of popular magazine articles: "Are You a Trapped Housewife?" "Are We the Last Married Generation?" "Happy Marriage, Is It Real?" "Can This Marriage Be Saved?" but it is also the casual talk at the Saturday night get-togethers and over the late morning cup of coffee that reveal the trends of the time. "Have you heard the news about the Meyers?" "Did you know Meg O'Brien has left Tom?" "But the Falcones seemed like such a perfect couple!" It is also the tearstained look on the face of a young mother as she drops off the 10-year-old at a Girl Scout meeting, the embarrassed explanations and last-minute cancellation of a dinner date: "Dick isn't feeling so well tonight," or the urgency of a friend's whispered request, "Could we get together for coffee sometime? I've really got to talk to somebody!"

Their names may be Brian and Andrea with a unique identity and a special history as a couple; they may live in a suburban neighborhood of a certain city, but their story is legion. All of us know a Brian and Andrea. They may be married 20 years or two, they may have four children or none, but they are our friends, our neighbors, our families, us. Something is happening to couples like Brian and Andrea that has never happened before to the degree and to the extent that it is occurring today.

None of this is to suggest that there are not strong, healthy families, nor is it to say that all marriages are failing. But some marriages—perhaps many marriages—are under severe stress, and others have been shattered. The most commonly quoted statistic is that one out of four marriages ends in divorce, but this figure says nothing about the other three marriages in that equation. Can it be assumed that these other marital relationships are necessarily "happy marriages" in the ordinary sense of that term?

More to the point is the research done several years ago at a Midwestern university. A large sampling of data seemed to indicate that out of every 12 marriages, four end in divorce. Another six of the 12 marriages were described as "utilitarian," the couple shared surface satisfactions, but had a relational "stand-off"—a union that is not fulfilling the human needs or providing the opportunities for growth of the men and women involved. Only two of every 12 marriages surveyed were described as "total"—"happy marriages" where a husband and wife were enriched as persons by their marital relationship.

Statistics look different when they are clothed in flesh and blood. In real life terms, every unhappy marriage can mean one broken home, two broken hearts. It can mean two unhappy and lonely people who have somehow failed to realize one of life's richest moments. It also implies children deprived of either the physical or psychological presence of parents and the stability and security of a supportive home environment during critical formative years. In time, the children of an unhappy marriage grow up to carry their insecurities and fears into their own marriages. Like a virus, failed marriages infect other human relationships in subsequent generations.

AN AMERICAN PHENOMENON?

The state of contemporary marriage, however, is not something new. A case could be made that marriage in America has been a very fragile thing right from the beginning. Americans, as a people, have always experienced great difficulty with close human relationships. Dr. Anthony T. Padovano sees evidence for this assertion in an American literature which has yet to produce any major work dealing with a successful relationship between a man and a woman, or even between two people.[1]

Curiously, many American creative works deal with people who are alone. In literature there is Washington Irving's Rip Van Winkle, Cooper's Natty Bumpo, Twain's Huckleberry Finn alone on a Mississippi raft, Melville's Captain Ahab in his mad, lonely pursuit of the great white whale in *Moby Dick;* Walt Whitman celebrates in *The Song of Myself,* and Emily Dickinson peeked out at the world from behind window curtains and composed poems about being alone. The great contemporary painter, Andrew Wyeth, who created the melancholy "Christina's World," almost always paints pictures of solitary people. On the movie screen as well, the classic Western depicts a lonely hero who speaks in monosyllables, relates to no one except his horse, and rides off into the sunset—alone.

The point is this: loneliness and alienation have been around for a long, long time. As a people, Americans have always had trouble relating to one another. It should come as no surprise, then, to discover some unstable marriages today, since the success or failure of the marital union ultimately depends upon the people involved and their ability to establish and maintain an intimate human relationship.

Cultural trends have also contributed to the in-

1. Anthony T. Padovano, *Facing Today's Prayer Problems,* a cassette, Conference-A-Month Club (Englewood, N.J., June 1973).

stability of contemporary marriage. Of the many social changes that have affected the face of marriage, none is more far-reaching than the loss of traditional family functions. In an older society, marriage provided many services that have now been taken over by other institutions. Family sociologists, taking their lead from the writing of William F. Ogburn, usually identify seven changing functions. *Survival,* for example, is one of them. The primitive Eskimo hunter really needs his wife in order to survive. She chews the seal skins and softens them into clothing for him to wear as protection against the Arctic cold. He shoots a polar bear to provide food for her to eat. They need each other. Without her, he freezes; without him, she starves. The same was also true on the American frontier, in the days of the wagon trails and the Indian raids. In suburban America, however, a person doesn't have to be married in order to survive. He buys food from the supermarket and protection from the local police.

Educational services are another area of marital change. In Revolutionary days, home and family were the place where one learned the three R's, as well as cultural values. Today the local Day Care Center, the school, and the television screen have taken over much of the educational function of the family.

In the past, the family also had the very crucial function of *conferring identity.* People were secure because they knew who they were and where they were from. The Broadway musical *Carnival* told the story of a young woman whose parents had died and who, completely alone, joined a traveling circus. In one scene, she thinks back nostalgically to the small town, Mira, where she was raised. Then she sings, "What I liked the best in Mira is—everybody knows my name!" Today, all this has changed. Cut off from ethnic roots, a family name doesn't count so much anymore as a source of personal identity.

SUCCESSFUL MARRIAGES

Marriage in America is very fragile; its functions have drastically changed through the years. And yet, a significant number of marriages are so successful that the social scientists and researchers describe them as "total" or "intrinsic" marriages. The source of this success seems to be the bond or the union that exists between the couple. They are comfortable with each other, content with life, and happy in their marriage. Dr. John F. Cuber and Mrs. Peggy B. Harroff, in their study, *The Significant Americans,* have some of the couples themselves describe their experience of the "intrinsic marriage." One wife described her second marriage with a marvelous metaphor:

> Well, we've got a marriage-type marriage. Do you know what I mean? So many people—and me in my first marriage—just sort of touch on the edges of existence—don't really marry. It's funny, but my cookbook distinguishes between marinating and marrying of flavors. You know, the marinated flavors retain their identity—just mix a little—or the one predominates strongly over the other. But the married ones blend into something really new and the separate identities are lost. Well, a lot of people that I know aren't married at all—just marinated![2]

A scientist in his early 50's had essentially the same view of marriage, but he described it differently:

> . . . Now that doesn't mean that we haven't differences—sometimes sharp ones—or that I haven't inhibited some desires because she doesn't want to share them. All I mean is that I just don't have or want to have any separate existence that amounts to anything. I do my work as well as I can, but—and I'm a little

2. John F. Cuber with Peggy B. Harroff, *The Significant Americans* (New York: Appleton-Century, 1965), pp. 132-133. Reprinted by permission of Hawthorn Books, Inc. All rights reserved.

ashamed when I realize it—it doesn't have the importance to me that people think it does. As far as I'm concerned the whole corporation can go to hell anytime if it infringes unduly on her, and especially on us, and the things that are precious to us. . . .[3]

What is the difference between these marriages and Brian and Andrea's marriage? Why do some marriages flourish and others fail? A woman writer, Amy Gross, believes the difference lies in a mysterious "X factor" that is present in some marriages, but absent in others:

My superstitious belief in the X factor leaves me unresponsive to the notion of "working at" marriage, which is a very popular and even religious notion right now. What a grim picture it brings to mind: a diligent couple gritting their teeth, listening in measured turns to each other without humor or delight. The work ethic should leave marriage alone. But "learning" to be married—a natural, evolutionary process —is attractive and makes sense, particularly . . . for those with a low pain threshold. . . . If marriage is like life, as a lot of people claim, it is also like a game, and you can learn to play a game. You can learn the moves and strategies and become a better player.[4]

Perhaps the X factor is not such a mystery after all. It might be that the quality of certain marriages is different because the couples are different. Some are motivated to learn and are able to grow; others are not.

NEW DIRECTIONS POSSIBLE

Can Andrea's and Brian's marriage be saved? At this critical juncture of their marital life, their growth

3. *Ibid.,* p. 134.
4. Amy Gross, "Learning to Be Married: Or, How to Love a Total Stranger," *Redbook,* May, 1976, p. 84.

as a couple and the very existence of their marriage will depend upon their desire to preserve that relationship and their ability to "shift gears"—adjust to changing roles and new directions.

This is not an easy thing to do. Sympathetic friends had urged Brian to take Andrea on a "second honeymoon," a trip to Hawaii, away from the children and family tensions. Brian suggested the vacation, but Andrea put the idea down, saying flatly, "It's too late for that, Brian." Andrea's mother, on a holiday visit, sensed the strained relationship and, in a confidential moment, tactfully suggested a Marriage Encounter to her daughter. Andrea, although indifferent in her feelings toward Brian, was concerned with the effect their difficulties were having on the emotional life of the children. She made inquiries among several couples active in Marriage Encounter. All were enthusiastic in sharing the many ways their marriages had been enriched by the Encounter weekends. Each couple was careful to point out, however, that the movement offered support toward making good marriages better—not therapy for troubled relationships.

Then Brian, grasping at the last straw, approached a marriage counselor at a local family life clinic. At first, he was embarrassed admitting something as personal as a failed marriage, but the counselor seemed to understand his embarrassment and accept his feelings. After a while, Brian began to feel more at ease and described as best he could the tensions between himself and Andrea. He added, with a sigh, "I'd give anything to know what went wrong!"

The counselor nodded understandingly, then assured Brian that most people, when they first seek marriage counseling, do not really know what is wrong and are almost never able to put their finger on the basic problem. The therapist described marriage counseling as something like an old-fashioned wagon wheel. On the outside rim of that wheel are all the surface symptoms, the common concerns that afflict many marriages from time to time—in-law troubles, drink, infidelity, financial difficulties, sexual adjustment or roles. No matter how many difficulties there may be upon the rim, or how unusual they may seem, they all lead down through the spokes to the hub around which the whole "marriage wheel" revolves.

"There are probably as many different names for the center of that wheel as there are family life educators and marriage counselors," said Brian's therapist. "Some describe this hub as 'expectations.' Many use the term 'maturity.' Others hold that the central support of marriage consists in a couple's ability 'to communicate and share their deepest feelings!' " He added that, when a marriage is successful, these three factors—realistic expectations, facility of communication, and the ability to love—always seem to be present. When a marriage fails, no matter how many different symptoms first surface, one or more of these three is always lacking.

At first, Andrea was indifferent to Brian's visits to the counselor. After several weeks, however, she began to sense a subtle change in his behavior. He seemed more aware of her; he genuinely appeared to be listening and—for the first time in many years—was hearing her feelings. Her curiosity aroused, Andrea asked if she could sit in on the next counseling session. Brian agreed. As she listened to Brian's conversation with his counselor, Andrea was surprised to discover a side of her husband she had never seen before, or had forgotten ever existed. Behind the good looks and the golf-club bravado was a human being frightened by the constant specter of failure.

At the next session, Andrea and Brian tried listening to each other's feelings with the therapist assisting from the sidelines. It wasn't too successful at first, for Brian became very defensive as Andrea began to vent her own feelings of frustration, and there were a few moments of mutual recrimination. This time, however, the hour ended with Brian beginning to discover, for the first time, what identity as a woman and as a person had come to mean to Andrea.

In the following weeks, hesitantly at first, Brian and Andrea began examining the expectations they had each brought to their marriage. Brian admitted that his ideal wife was modeled on the "Mrs. Clean" role of his mother who was a compulsive housekeeper. Andrea began to sense that her early attraction to Brian contained a lot of idealism about her own father. At times, the counselor used a blackboard to diagram their relationship in terms of Transactional Analysis—the "I'm O.K., You're O.K." personality theory. "That's why you turned down the 'second honeymoon,' " explained Brian. "Daddy was buying off his child with a present!" "Exactly," answered Andrea, "I'm an adult, not your good little girl!"

In private sessions with the counselor, Andrea explored the meaning of growth in her own life. She came to understand that her reaching out for the attentions of other men was somehow tied in with her own struggle for identity, her feelings of inadequacy as a person, her needs to be recognized as a woman. She learned how she could be fulfilled and, at the same time, responsible for the other people in her life. Brian, for his part, began to see her as a person, not in a stereotyped way as a live-in housekeeper, but as a new woman with new roles and a new life.

WILLING TO GROW

Some months have passed and Brian and Andrea are still together. At the suggestion of their family therapist, they drew up a marriage contract to help redefine roles and responsibilities, but now it doesn't seem to be so necessary. Brian is still compulsive about his legal practice, more than Andrea would like, but he is able to share his business—and his fears—with her these days, and he genuinely respects Andrea's opinions and advice. They play an occasional game of golf together, but Brian is home more often and has begun to accept his role as father of the family. He encourages Andrea in her new career as a fashion consultant and takes more responsibility around the house—giving baths, babysitting, preparing meals, and, yes, doing housework.

Andrea and Brian haven't solved all their problems—and they still see their counselor from time to time—but both consider their marriage eminently more satisfying. They have begun to grow—together.

The written word "crisis" in Chinese combines two other ideographs—one means "danger," the other "opportunity." So it is with marriage. As couples such as Brian and Andrea pass from one phase of married life to another, there will certainly be times for serious stress, difficult periods of adjustment. These crises can sometimes mean the breakup of the marriage, or they can become an opportunity for a man and a woman to revitalize their relationship and renew their commitment to each other. Contemporary marriage brings many crises, but it also offers the opportunity for rich and lasting growth, if two people are willing to recognize not only danger, but opportunity, and to do something constructive about the crisis that results.

Chapter 2
Impossible Dreams

And as they rode off into the sunset, the Prince promised her his love, his riches and his castle in the clouds if only she would be his. She agreed. Later, after the wedding, they discussed the running of the kingdom. ". . . the castle is in terrible disarray," explained the Prince. "It needs the hand of a fine woman like yourself to straighten its many rooms and dust its many nooks and light its many fires and clean its many chimneys and sweep its many corridors and feed its many occupants and visitors. Then, we shall have many sons so that they may run the kingdom long after I am gone. I can only hope that when they come of age, they will be as lucky as I in finding a good wife." And with that they kissed and the Prince lived happily ever after . . . You've come a long way, baby!

This Virginia Slims advertisement depicts in a humorous way the differing dreams, hopes and expectations a man and woman bring with them to their marriage. The Prince may have lived happily ever after, but what about the Princess? Did she expect to spend her future days straightening rooms, dusting nooks, sweeping corridors and feeding visitors? What were *her* dreams of the future? Were they the same as those of her new husband?

Family Life educators and marriage counselors may differ when they name the most important factors that make for a happy marriage, but almost all agree that expectations—future dreams—on the part of both the bride and groom are high on the list of items that make for the success or failure of many marriages. In fact, the theory that differing expectations account for all or most of the difficulties in the early days of marriage has intrigued family counselors and sociologists for years. All too frequently, it seems, marital discord begins the day a partner discovers his or her mate does not match the expectations of yesterday.

In the ad, it was Prince Charming who dreamed those impossible dreams. For evidence indicates that men become disillusioned with marriage sooner than women because the male dreams of the future more unrealistically than the female. In any event, the death of dreams, on the part of either the husband or the wife, will soon affect the other partner, and the marriage relationship will begin to go sour. Prince Charming loses his magic charms; Cinderella, his Princess, turns back into a scullery maid as the clock strikes midnight on romance. Once, they both thought they were in love. Now, they feel like total strangers. She will say, "He just isn't the man I thought he was." He will say, "She is a different woman than the one I dated and married." Unrealistic expectations can bring about the end of many beautiful dreams. Wedding bells may toll the death of love.

When people fly to Europe for a vacation, or leave to visit a friend or a relative across the continent, they usually take with them some luggage for their trip—a flight bag and a small suitcase. While we all like to travel light, most people realize that a long-distance trip or a vacation always means carrying a certain amount of baggage. In the same way, although not nearly as obvious, men and women bring with them some social and psychic "baggage" as they begin their journey together into married life. This personal "baggage" is made up of many things: unique human identity, family history, past experiences, future fantasies and, sometimes, even fears.

DETERMINING FACTORS

What determines the kinds of dreams people pack into their suitcases as they begin their journey into marriage? There are several factors:

1. *Culture.* The climate in which a couple live—the culture that surrounds them—has a lot to do with their expectations. In contemporary America, the mass media strongly influence people even without their realizing it. Movies, magazines and especially television wreak havoc. Dr. Thomas A. Harris has described the dream-world of many couples:

> . . . they borrow a concept of marriage from the highly romanticized fiction they read, wherein husband has a nice job as a junior executive in a large advertising company and comes home every night with a bouquet of roses to a slender, radiant wife awaiting him in the fifty-thousand-dollar home with Armstrong floors and sparkling windows, in which the candles are lit and the stereo is playing music to make love by.[1]

Popular male and female media models also contribute to this sense of illusion. A young woman may know that her one and only doesn't have Paul Newman's blue eyes, but in her fantasies, consciously or uncon-

---

1. Thomas A. Harris, M.D., *I'm O.K., You're O.K.* (New York: Harper & Row, Publishers, Inc., 1969), p. 127.

sciously, the man in her life will be expected to have all the cool, the decisiveness, the masculinity of this popular male actor. She will want him to be as sexy as Robert Redford, as smart as Ralph Nader, as dedicated as Dan Rather, as cool as Joe Namath. But in real life, he will leave his socks on the floor, grow fat around the middle, fall asleep in front of the television and, as the years go on, be as romantic, understanding and tender as, perhaps, Archie Bunker. The *Playboy* centerfold, the jet-set swinger and the *Cosmopolitan* cover girl make up the dream wife of many American males. She is expected to be mistress, mother, beauty queen, career woman, child psychologist, gourmet cook, Bunny hostess and perfect housekeeper all rolled into one—a cross between Gloria Steinem, Cher Bono Allman, Mary Tyler Moore, Raquel Welch, Betty Furness, Jane Fonda and Joyce Brothers. Reality dawns, and impossible dreams fade the day a new husband discovers that marriage to a woman also means very human things like hair rollers and bunny slippers, blue days and sudden moods, a bathroom hung with pantyhose and a vacuum cleaner running during the sudden death overtime of a pro football game.

2. *Family History.* The climate of a person's home and the quality of the relationship with parents also have a lot to do in determining types of expectations. "I'm never going to marry when I grow up," a teenage woman once said in a counseling session. "I've been watching my own parents' marriage for 17 years and all they ever do is argue and fight." An extreme example, perhaps, but the kind of relationship a man or woman has with his or her own parents, the models seen at home, colors to a great extent the kind of behavior expected from a future mate.

Such was the case of Evelyn Baum's relationship with her husband in Ruth Harris' novel, *Decades.* Evelyn had come to a crisis in her marriage. With the help of a therapist, she began to gain some insight into the ways her own family background had contributed to her present problems with her husband, Nat:

> Evelyn examined her inability to have more children, her consequent frigidity and the effect it must have had on Nat. She was astounded to learn that she expected the same things from her husband that she had taken for granted from her father: total loyalty on his part and complete subservience on hers. She wanted him to be the daddy and herself to be the child. It was the first time Evelyn had realized that, and she said in amazement, "But fathers and husbands are different!"[2]

Fathers and husbands are different; so are mothers and daughters. In the course of her therapy, Evelyn also discovered how her relationship with her mother had had a great influence on her failures with her own daughter, Joy:

> She was surprised when she realized that her relationship with Joy duplicated the relationship she had had with her own mother. Evelyn and her mother had been, at the most, distant relatives. Never once had they had an intimate conversation. Never once had they confided in each other the realities of their lives. Evelyn's mother was a mystery to Evelyn, and she realized she must be a mystery to Joy. The only difference had been that Evelyn was brought up at a time when children took it for granted that they were to respect their parents and Joy grew up at a time when children took it for granted that they were to hate and defy their parents openly. Other than that, both mother-daughter relationships, with Evelyn in the middle, were characterized by distance, detachment and a complete lack of intimacy.[3]

2. Ruth Harris, *Decades* (New York: Simon and Schuster, The New American Library, 1974), p. 222. Reprinted by permission of the publisher.
3. *Ibid.,* p. 221-222.

3. *Unconscious Needs.* In American society there are many "walking wounded"—people struggling toward maturity and working through the unfulfilled needs of their past. Sometimes, even without realizing it, such men and women perceive marriage as a way of satisfying these basic human needs.

Harry, for example, was an only child. His father was a busy doctor, his mother a professional woman whose career always came first. Harry's relationship with his parents, especially with his mother because it lacked warmth and affection, was cool and distant. Unable to establish close friendships, he would be best described, during his first two years in college, as a "loser." Awkward in manner, backward in dress, Harry's very demeanor invited rejection.

Joyce was the eldest daughter of a large, lower-middle-class family. Surrounded by so many younger brothers and sisters, Joyce from her early teenage years had been a second mother in her busy home. She enjoyed college, but her interests were more domestic than those of her more socially minded suite mates and as a result, Joyce rarely dated.

One day, in the college cafeteria, Harry met Joyce. It was, as they say, love at first sight. For the first time ever, Harry found a woman who would break through his wall of isolation and loneliness, accept his inadequacies and failures, give direction to his life. Joyce, on her part, felt good to be needed. In Harry, she discovered someone she could comfort and console, upon whom she could lavish love and tender care. Harry needed a mother; Joyce had found her little lost boy. Need had responded to need. Their married life will be based, to a large extent, upon these mutual needs and role expectations.

Culture, family or need create a situation where many couples' expectations can *differ,* where some can be *excessive* and others can be *confused.*

DIFFERING EXPECTATIONS

"Cynthia was so romantic when we were dating,"
says Dominick, "that I thought after our marriage that
she'd be even more responsive sexually, but some days
she's about as warm as an iceberg. Besides, I didn't
mind the suggestions she used to make about my
clothes, but all she seems to do now is nag about my
appearance." "I'm no prude," responds Cynthia, "but
love means tenderness, not just always being treated as
a sex object. And as far as his clothes are concerned,
Dominick knew the way a man dresses had always meant
a lot to me!"

No one ever completely understands another person,
but more people marry today than ever before from
different backgrounds—different cultures, different
religions, different ethnic and national origins, different
economic backgrounds. Men and women differ biologi-
cally; so, too, do their values, sexual attitudes, social
customs, emotional needs, and role expectations. And
these differing expectations, if unrecognized or
unresolved, can lead to marital discord.

Expectations are excessive, or unrealistic, when
either the husband or wife, or both, expects more from
the partner or the relationship than is realistically
possible. When Prince Charming told his bride that his
castle needed a woman to dust its many nooks, light
its many fires, and clean its many chimneys, he was
revealing more about his own role expectations than
he was about those of his new wife. He was saying, in
effect, that he perceived woman's role in marriage to be
exclusively that of a housekeeper and mother. Given
the fact of woman's emerging roles in contemporary
society, how realistic is the Prince's narrow view? What
if his bride's own role expectations are different? Was
Evelyn realistic in expecting Nat to be a carbon copy
of her father? What if he was unwilling or unable to ful-
fill her secret dreams, what then?

Expectations are confused when couples lack a clear understanding of the goals of their marriage, especially a contemporary understanding of marital happiness. Young couples in a family life course, or Pre-Cana conference, when asked what is the one thing they want most out of marriage, will almost always reply, in one way or another, that they want "to be happy." Dr. Richard H. Klemer has stated that the primary reason for the fragility of marriage today is that happiness has replaced stability as a major goal.[4] Certainly, people should see married life as a way of achieving human happiness; indeed, one of the readings in the old marriage liturgy used to promise the bride and groom that their marriage would bring "the fullest measure of earthly happiness allotted to man in this vale of tears."

But the *meaning* of happiness has many couples confused today. As Richard Klemer observes:

> . . . this happiness is often expected to come with the marriage. Since it is no longer absolutely necessary for people to spend their entire lives grubbing out a marginal existence, happiness *is* a more realistic goal than it ever was before. The important question, though, is how that happiness is achieved. If each partner is expecting to receive bountiful happiness from the marriage without giving anything to it, someone is bound to be disappointed. For marriage is a giving relationship—especially after the children arrive. This has not changed. It is as true today as it was a hundred years age.[5]

Because people today have been taught to believe that their lives will be better if they buy a better car, a better stereo, a better toothpaste, they tend to think of marital happiness as a product that offers prepackaged

4. Richard H. Klemer, *Marriage and Family Relationships* (New York: Harper & Row, Publishers, Inc., 1970) p. 22.
5. *Ibid.,* p. 23.

satisfaction in return for the price of a wedding license. Unlike consumer goods, however, happiness is a human experience that is achieved only by those couples who are willing to make a personal investment into their ongoing union and who work together in the task of deepening that relationship. Even the Constitution of the United States guarantees, not happiness, but *the pursuit* of happiness.

SHARING EXPECTATIONS

The most important aspect in a marriage relationship, then, is not the expectations, but the two people who dream those dreams; not their fantasies for the future, but the couple's sharing of their lives today. It is critically important, therefore, that a man and a woman preparing for marriage, or a couple already married, find an opportunity, from time to time, for an honest sorting out of the expectations they both bring to their union.

This mutual sharing of expectations can be done in a *formal* setting. Many premarriage courses now provide this opportunity for the engaged. For married couples, husband and wife expectations can be shared at a Marriage Encounter, at a weekend retreat or by a conference with an understanding counselor.

Sometimes these expectations can be identified even more honestly by the couple themselves in an *informal* way. *Crisis situations* offer an excellent opportunity. Suppose a couple have had an argument because one or the other is too tired or too busy or came home too late to give the two-year-old daughter a bath before putting her to bed. After the argument subsides, but before its origins are forgotten, it helps for both a man and his wife to write a paragraph or a list entitled, "What happened to me in the last 24 hours that led to this scene?" They then can compare: problems you caused for me, problems I caused for you, what I expected of you, what I think you expected of me.

Another way to bring expectations out into the open is by playing "Possible Alternatives," a simple projective technique that is as easy as a parlor game. Let's suppose (a couple might say) that by our 10th anniversary we aren't able to have any children. What will our marriage be like? What do I see my role to be, given that possibility. What will be my husband's or my wife's role? The couple then compare their possible futures. There are, of course, any number of variables to this game: What if we don't own our own home? What if the husband is out of work and supported by his wife? What if one of our babies is an "exceptional" child? What if one of our mothers is widowed? What if one of us decides to go back to college, or work for a graduate degree? What will be the wife's role? What will be the husband's?

The important thing about "Possible Alternatives" is not so much specific solutions or strategies, but the expectations for the future that it reveals. Uncovering the deeper values and priorities behind the choices each partner makes is more important than "instant answers" to marriage problems.

Still another way for a couple to share their future realistically is by an *Expectations Inventory.* Each partner answers the questions below from his or her own point of view only. Each tries to be as honest and objective as he/she can in responding to each item:

EXPECTATIONS INVENTORY

1. Ten years from now, I would want the following statement to be true:

a. We will be living in the
  ☐ country
  ☐ suburb
  ☐ small town

☐ medium city
☐ large city
☐ other ——————

b. We will be living in a:
☐ house
☐ apartment
☐ trailer
☐ commune
☐ other ——————

c. We will be earning:
☐ $10,000 a year
☐ $15,000 a year
☐ $20,000 a year
☐ $25,000 a year
☐ $50,000 a year
☐ other ——————

2. If my spouse had a job that kept him or her away from home seven days out of each month, I:
☐ could not tolerate it
☐ could tolerate it only if it was temporary
☐ would be somewhat concerned, but could tolerate it
☐ would not be concerned

3. If we had $500 to spend on a two-week vacation, I would like to —————— and do ——————; if we had children, I:
☐ would want to take them
☐ would not want to take them

4. In 10 years your father-in-law dies and your spouse asks you if you have objections to having your mother-in-law move in with you indefinitely. Your reaction would be:
☐ yes, I have objections
☐ no, I do not have objections
☐ maybe, if ——————

5. We should have ———— children when our family is complete.

6. True — False — The mother of preschool children should *not* be employed or separated from the children during the day.

7. True — False — The woman of a married team should be the one who leaves her job to raise preschool children even if she has a larger income than the man.

8. True — False — In a mature marriage relationship, a man or a woman should be able to have close single friends of the opposite sex.

9. True — False — Sexual fulfillment in marriage means making love at least three or four times a week.

10. True — False — We should never move farther than a day's drive from our parents and family.

11. True — False — Camping, hiking, snowmobiling, fishing, etc., are my favorite recreational activities.

12. True — False — It is essential to have a large shopping mall less than an hour's drive from where we live.

13. True — False — A wife should have her own checking account.

14. True — False — If a wife has a full-time job outside the home, the housework (cooking, cleaning, mar-

keting, laundry, etc.) should be equally divided between the husband and wife.

15. True — False — A woman, if she is so inclined, should be able to complete or continue her education, do volunteer work or take a part-time job after marriage.

16. True — False — Fathers should take an *active* role in the care (diapering, bathing, disciplining, etc.) of the children.

Comparing the answers together is as important to the success of the *Expectations Inventory* as answering the questions. There are no "right" or "wrong" solutions to the questionnaire. What is important are the values, the expectations for the future those answers reveal.

So the Prince and the Princess rode off into the sunset together. Whether the next day will dawn sunny and warm or cloudy and gray is determined, to a great extent, by the realism of the expectations both bring to their marriage. Future dreams or frightening night-mares, honest hopes or frustrated fancies, the happiness of their tomorrow depends upon the sharing of their mutual expectations of roles, responsibilities and marital priorities today.

Chapter 3
Silent Words, Unspoken Feelings[1]

Angie and Fred did a lot of talking with each other before their marriage. Conversation came quite easily about their common interests—friends, sex, movies, sports and, especially, the future. So much to say, so many things to share.

Fred is a young teacher; Angie works as a secretary in an office. They have been married now for several months, and this weekend they plan to drive over to her parents for Sunday night supper. So Angie asks, it seems quite casually, "Why don't you wear your new sweater and slacks up to Mom's?" His sweatshirt and jeans may be fine for the apartment, but since her parents have yet to accept Fred completely, Angie wants him to look his best.

Fred, like a lot of men, grew up taking words at their face value. So when asked about dressing up, he doesn't hear Angie's embarrassment, just the simple question. Fred, putting down the sports page, responds to Angie's words, rather than to her feelings and answers,

1. Material for this chapter has been adapted from an article previously published in *MARRIAGE and Family Living*, March, 1976.

"Oh, we're only going up to your mother's . . . these clothes are good enough!"

Since Angie has a message behind her words, and probably, as a woman, is more sensitive to feeling tones, she now hears something in Fred's reply that really isn't there. When Fred answers absently, that "these are good enough" for what seems to him an informal occasion, Angie thinks she hears him saying, "I'm going to wear these clothes whether you like it or not and I don't give a damn about your feelings or your mother's!" Angie begins to cry. Fred asks what's wrong. Angie answers, "Nothing." Fred sits there, wondering what he said, mumbling that he'll never understand women.

Most couples entering marriage believe they can communicate perfectly. They keep talking the first few weeks and months and then, for some, a crisis comes as it did in the case of Fred and Angie, and communication breaks down completely. For other couples, the change is more gradual, more subtle. Conversation doesn't come as easily as it did before. There seems to be nothing to talk about. Boredom slowly sets in. Ruth Harris pictures the gradual erosion of intimacy between one husband and wife, Nat and Evelyn:

> Nat used to talk to her by the hour when they were first married and he confided his dreams and ambitions, his fears and insecurities. They would stay up half the night holding each other and talking about themselves and their future, but now, if Nat had any dreams or ambitions, fears or insecurities, Evelyn didn't know what they were because he didn't tell her about them. When Evelyn asked why he didn't talk to her anymore, Nat simply denied that he had stopped.

> "I talk to you all the time," he said.

> Evelyn was lost for an answer. Yes, they talked about whether the car needed servicing, wheth-

er it was time to have storm windows put up,
if they should buy a new tube for the old Du-
mont or buy a new television set altogether,
how many times a month the service should
mow the lawn, and what train Nat would be taking. The things they talked about did not make
Evelyn feel that she was intimate with her husband. Slowly and surely and helplessly, Evelyn
saw that their lives were separating.[2]

Why does this subtle decay in communication
happen? What is it that goes wrong? Some of the reasons are *cultural.* The conversation of children gives
a clue. Little girls tend to talk about their friends,
whom they like in class, what the teacher said to Betty,
Sally's new dress, and so on. Little boys, on the other
hand, carry on conversations about sports, mechanical
and spatial things. Different conditioning as children
creates a situation in which the two sexes sometimes
discover they have little in common to talk about as
adults.

Traditional roles can also create a communications
gap. Men go to work and spend their day talking to
other adults. By the very nature of things, they want a
little peace and quiet when they get home. Their wives,
if they don't work outside the home, are alone all day
without companionship. They are eager to start talking
as soon as their husbands walk in the door.

A lot of *ignorance* prevents many men and women
from understanding the whys and ways of communicating.
Marriage is the first time most people, like Fred and
Angie, have ever experienced an intimate relationship.
They may talk quite freely, but real communication is a
far different and much more difficult thing. Besides
words, it means attending to feeling tones, to nonverbals,
and to body language.

2. Ruth Harris, *Decades* (New York: Simon and Schuster, The New
   American Library, 1974), pp. 190-191. Reprinted by permission of
   publisher.

DIFFERENT KINDS OF COMMUNICATION

The first step is to recognize the difference between *verbal* and *nonverbal* communication. *Verbal* means the message transmitted by the words—"I'd like a cup of coffee"; "It's 11:00 o'clock"; "Where's the front page of the newspaper?" These are the kinds of simple messages, with words, we send one another every day. We are always talking, so verbal communication appears to be the most significant way by which we communicate with one another. But it really isn't, because research indicates only 30% of our communication is verbal! That means 70% of the messages we send one another are without words or by *nonverbal* communication.

Nonverbal communication can happen in a number of different ways. Sometimes it can be the *feeling tone* behind the words that sends the real message. For example, a certain college chaplain has genius for getting his Newman program and his picture in the newspapers and on the media. Once he even made the front page of the *New York Times* Sunday Sports Section. Soon after, a friend called him on the phone and began the conversation by saying, "Charlie, you old so and so, you've done it again!" The chaplain was pleased by the call because he heard the speaker's feelings of admiration and esteem. If a bishop were addressed with the same earthy phrase, however, the reaction might be far different! Clearly, then, an expression can have a meaning quite different from the content of the words. That is why a woman will sometimes cry when a man says he loves her, because what she's really hearing is the flat, bored, uncaring feelings behind his words. Or, a woman can say to a man, after he's pulled some practical joke or surprised her with a particularly extravagant gift, "I hate you" so lovingly that he knows the words are not those of hostility, but rather of tenderness.

Body language is another form of nonverbal communication. Baseball fans have been watching body language for years without even knowing it. The umpire has made a close call at home plate, the manager comes running from the dugout, and immediately the umpire crosses his arms in front of his chest—his way of sending a message without words that he's in a fixed position from which he won't retreat, or that he's protecting himself from an attack.

In thousands of different ways we all send silent messages to each other. Couples preparing for marriage have their own special set of signals. A woman drags her unwilling fiance to a premarriage course. He slumps in his chair, stares at the ceiling, or puts his hands behind his head — his way of saying to the Pre-Cana director, "I'm not buying this" or "You've got to show me." Married couples also have their own private language, as Anne Roiphe describes it:

> A man and woman have many silent ways of signaling. A particular woman may gain weight or let the gray in her hair show when she wants some attention she may not be able to ask for directly. A man takes up golf and brings home friends when he doesn't enjoy long hours with his wife any more. A woman cooks a man's favorite dish by way of sending him a love note. A man may plan a vacation, buy theater tickets or extend the patio as a way of expressing love to his wife. He may be tired all the time, or reading all the time, or be out with male friends. All are ways of telling his wife, "I'm pulling away. I can't help it, but I'm drifting off."[3]

The most profound nonverbal communication of all is sex. "I wanted to make love to her," a young husband says in a counseling session, "but she told me 'not tonight,' so I turned over and tried to go to sleep. She sat up half the night crying." The young wife cried because her husband had not read the real message. She

3. Anne Roiphe, "The Private Language of Marriage," McCall's, Feb. 1974, p. 128.

felt she should have been so irresistible that he would have persisted despite all obstacles!

The way a husband comes in the front door, sits at the kitchen table and says "Hi"; the way a wife holds her head, puts the dishes on the table, smiles or frowns: all of these are forms of communication. Seventy per cent of the messages between men and women are sent in this way. Some people are so sensitive to nonverbal communication that they can tell when a friend has told a lie, or they pick up vibrations, even in a glance across a room, from people they've never met. Sometimes these same people, however, aren't as sensitive to nonverbal messages in a marriage relationship, either because their signals have become so familiar that they cease to convey meaning, or because they block nonverbal messages they find difficult to accept.

Are there "Five Rules for More Effective Communication" or "Instant Intimacy in Three Easy Lessons"? Pop psychology can sometimes satisfy the "how to" hunger of modern marrieds, but only at the price of a terribly painful self-consciousness. Anne Roiphe has likened the effects of a marital "easy-answers" approach to questioning a centipede. He walked easily and gracefully, but when he was asked how he coordinated the movement of his many legs, he realized he'd never thought about it before and was unable to take another step![4] Ms. Roiphe also criticizes an excessive concern for techniques:

> When people speak of communication between marriage partners, I now see IBM machines banging out messages on punch cards. Large corporations concern themselves with communications; advertisers speak of communication with the public; media men manipulate communications. Communications belong to technology. Men and women in bed together do

4. *Ibid.*, p. 83.

better to talk and make love, to fight, to sulk, to stroke, to whisper and laugh and to leave the communicating to public-relations men and financial analysts.[5]

IMPROVING RESPONSE

What follows, therefore, are not "easy answers" to more effective marital communications, but merely commonsense suggestions to improve the ways we respond to the most important people in our lives:

1. *Be aware of feelings.* It is important to hear the feeling tone behind the words people use in significant conversations. This doesn't mean that every time a wife asks her husband what he wants for supper, he should say to himself: "I wonder what she meant by that?" It does mean, however, that he should listen much more than usual with what Theodore Reik calls the "third ear." All of us should try to respond to a person's feelings if they are different from the words used.

A mother once missed an opportunity to respond this way to her 11-year-old son, Bob. Just before they went for a ride to the store, his dad had bawled the boy out for something he had forgotten to do. As he got in the car, Bob said, as every little boy has complained at one time or another, "Everybody around this house hates me." His mother should have responded to his feelings by answering, "Seems like nobody cares about you, right?" Instead, she answered his words, tried to reassure him by saying, "Oh, we all love you, Bob." The result was that he wasn't reassured. Mother and son drove to the store in silence and a precious moment had passed.

In the same way, in many of the most significant moments of marriage, people will use words they really don't mean. If they don't hear the hidden feelings, and

5. *Ibid.,* p. 128.

respond only to the words, they will miss many rich moments of opportunity in life. A husband finds his wife brooding in front of the bathroom mirror because she has just discovered two gray hairs. For the first time in her life, she feels old, her youth beginning to fade. Some husbands might react by saying, "Well, if it bothers you so much, why don't you dye your hair?" An understanding man, however, will respond with words borrowed from a familiar commercial, "Honey, you're not getting older, you're getting better!"

We should hear the feeling tone behind our own words; if we want to communicate, we should be in touch with our own feelings and be willing to share them verbally. Whether we know it or not, whether we intend it or not, we are already communicating most of those feelings nonverbally, if they are negative feelings. If feelings are repressed, if we pretend they don't exist, not only will they be communicated without words, but negative feelings can fester within, assume a proportion they don't deserve, and ultimately cause a whole relationship to deteriorate.

A university family life course requires that couples, as a "take-home" assignment after a communications workshop, share with each other one feeling they never before revealed. Sometimes the results are startling. One future bride finally summoned up the courage to reveal to her husband-to-be her very negative feelings about his sister. A casual observer might consider such a revelation trivial, but the woman's feelings were very real and very deep. Her relationship with her future husband will be more honest, communication in their marriage easier, now that these feelings are finally out in the open.

2. *Communication breaks down when we send conflicting messages.* "Tony, are you listening to me?" his wife asks, and Tony, sitting in front of the T.V. set, his back to his wife, eyes glued to the fourth quarter of

the Super Bowl, replies, "Yeah, I'm listening, I'm listening." A conflicting message happens when verbal and nonverbal communications contradict each other.

Family therapist Virginia Satir has observed that the troubled families she has counseled have all handled their communication in the style of Tony's double-meaning message.[6] When a person hears a double message, Satir suggests four possible ways to respond: listen to the words and ignore the nonverbals; react to the nonverbals and ignore the words; ignore the whole message; or, lastly, advert to the fact that we are hearing a double meaning and say we are confused.

Of these four ways of responding, only the second and the fourth encourage continued communication. So, sometimes, it is better to ignore the words and respond directly to the feeling tone — as the mother should have done on the way to the store with her son. Or, a person can advert to the fact that he or she is receiving a mixed message by responding, "I'm confused, because I think I am hearing two things." When replying in this way, however, one should be very sensitive to the feelings of the other, because some people won't admit even to themselves that they are sending a double message!

3. *Good communication needs a climate of trust.* The plant craze is upon us! Begonias, philodendrons, coleus, ivy! They're crawling all over our homes and even hanging from the windows of our offices! We take good care of our plants — just a certain amount of water, not too much sun and only the right kind of soil. Plants do need a proper climate to grow. But we often overlook something as precious, and as fragile — communication between two friends or a husband and wife can also happen only with the right kind of "soil," the right climate. The soil of communication is security;

6. Virginia Satir, *Peoplemaking* (Palo Alto: Science and Behavior Books, 1972), p. 59.

its climate, trust. Feelings are like fragile flowers. If they are not accepted or, worse yet, if they are exposed to the icy winds of open rejection, they soon wither and fade. Sometimes they never blossom again.

Fear is the great inhibitor of communication. Some people don't share feelings because they fear rejection. Others reject what is said to them because they are afraid of the words they hear, perceiving them as a threat to their security. Then there is the fear of starting an argument, the fear of hurting another's feelings, the fear of losing someone's love.

Dr. Richard Klemer has noted that while wives complain that husbands hesitate to share feelings, many husbands will assert, in counseling sessions, that the sharing of feelings only causes them more trouble. Either their wives reject their feelings as being inadequate, or accept them for a time, but use the feelings against them at a later date.[7]

There may also be cultural reasons why the American male finds it so hard to let down his defense long enough to share feelings. The climate of mistrust and suspicion that exists in some offices and industries is frightening, if not downright dehumanizing. One national organization, for example, serves two different meals at its annual sales banquet. Salesmen who made their yearly quota dine on lobster and sirloin; those who didn't eat franks and beans. For husbands working eight hours a day, five days a week, under such emotional pressure and in such a climate of mistrust, it is difficult to trust at home. Given these conditions, some husbands find it impossible, at the end of the day, to reveal their deepest feelings to their wives.

When St. John the Baptist first appeared, people asked him, "Are you the one who is to come, or should we look for another?" We hunger in our hearts, all of us,

7. Richard H. Klemer, *Marriage and Family Relationships* (New York: Harper & Row, 1970), p. 213.

for acceptance and approval. We long to find someone who will understand us, accept us as we are, with all our faults and failings. So we search the faces of all those we meet, looking for some faint flicker of love and understanding, saying, in effect, "Are you the one who is to come? The one who will accept me as I am, the one person whom I really can trust?" If this kind of acceptance and trust is ever to be found in this world, then it should be the one gift couples offer each other. Without it, communication can never happen!

4. *Honest communication implies discretion.* One final question: does effective communication in marriage mean that a man and woman be totally and completely honest and open and share *all* their feelings with each other? Marriage experts have often exalted honesty as a marital virtue, and most people would be inclined to say "yes" — a husband and wife should be able to share anything.

But honesty is a two-edged sword that can cut both ways. One side clears tension, brings feelings out into the open; it helps a couple see each other as they really are, enabling them to put aside the Halloween masks of childhood and infantile games. The other side is the cutting edge of honesty—brutal frankness—which can sometimes be nothing less than a facade for aggression, or verbal violence.

Total sharing of feelings, complete honesty and openness is an ideal, but it presupposes very mature, self-actualized people. In the real world, most of us still bear a lot of scars; we are still vulnerable. This is why Jesus was careful not to reveal everything all at once to his apostles; why he told them, "I have many things to say to you, but you cannot bear them all now."

In an intimate relationship, such as marriage, we come to know each other's vulnerabilities, our sore spots. Therefore the more loving thing, at times, is not to communicate in certain areas, even when we are asked to do so by those we love. A birthday gift for a wife may be the wrong color and in a style more suited for her mother-in-law, but for her to say that in so many words can cause unnecessary pain and could reject a well-intentioned desire of her husband to please. A husband may have a healthy, professional relationship with his secretary — he may admire her real business acumen — but he will be careful not to praise her too much at home if his wife finds this relationship hard to accept.

REAL HEARING BUILDS TRUST

There are no shortcuts to effective communication. It only happens when a couple make an honest effort and attempt to hear each other's feelings, create a climate of trust, and mean what they say. Once, the old Jewish prophet Elijah was hiding from his enemies in a cave. He was told to be ready for "the Lord will be passing by." This is how the bible then describes what happened:

> . . . A stormy and heavy wind was rending the mountain and crushing rocks before the Lord — but the Lord was not in the wind. After the wind was an earthquake, but the Lord was not in the earthquake. After the earthquake, there there was fire — but the Lord was not in the fire. And after the fire, a still, small voice . . . When Elijah heard it, he hid his face in his cloak and went out and stood at the entrance of the cave . . ." (1 Kgs 19: 11-13).

The "still, small voice" of God heard by Elijah is like the role played by communication in marriage. A couple's marriage may be buffeted by violent storms from without; the winds of change may sweep through society, threatening to crush even the most secure relationship between a man and a woman; but the thing that makes the difference and will enable a marriage to survive is the bond, the union that exists between a husband and a wife — the word spoken between them, that "still, small voice," that whispers their ability to communicate.

Words comfort, words heal. Words cause laughter and bring about joy. Words inspire hope and invoke care. Words say good-bye in the morning and hello at the day's end. Words cry in moments of great sorrow, and casual words curl themselves before the fire. But the most precious words of all are those spoken between a man and a woman. They are, indeed, the sounds of silence — the "still, small voice" that says in a hundred different ways, the words no one ever tires of hearing, "I love you."

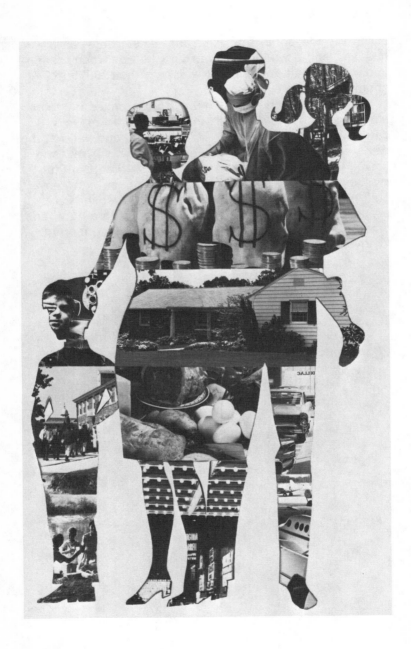

Chapter 4
On the Dotted Line . . .

The New Yorker magazine once featured a cartoon
of an upper-class Westchester wedding. The setting
was a family garden: parents in morning dress and full-
length gowns, the smiling minister in surplice and stole.
The bride, by contrast, wore a granny dress with flowers
in her newly frizzled hair. The groom was dressed in
buckskins and beads. Together the young couple
solemnly pledged "in all times and in all places to con-
demn war, pollution and nonbiodegradable containers,
to support the Third World and to fight for a better life
for the migrant farmworker"!

Statements about war, pollution and the Third World
may never replace traditional marriage vows in most
ceremonies, but some couples today are drawing up
detailed contracts before they walk down the aisle.
Written agreements spelling out marital rights and duties,
roles and responsibilities, are becoming increasingly
popular, not only for newlyweds, but for couples already
married. Jacqueline Kennedy and the late Aristotle
Onassis are reported to have written such an agreement
covering 170 items of their married life.

Marriage contracts detail the whole range of the

husband and wife relationship—money, housework, sex,
children, even infidelity. Some agreements are very
specific "job descriptions"; ". . . Diane will cook all
dinners except Sunday supper. Brad prepares Sunday
supper and any other meals on his 'duty' nights if Diane
isn't home. The person inviting friends in for supper
does the shopping, cooking and the dinner dishes. If
the invitation comes from both Brad and Diane, the dinner
duties will be shared equally. . . ."

For example, Greg and Carol, a young couple, drew
up a contract after several years of marriage. Greg is
an engineer; Carol, a copywriter in an advertising agency
who continued working after marriage. The first years
of their wedded life were idyllic: two-bedroom apartment in a wooded suburban development; quiet evenings
together after work when they dined by candlelight
and shared together the small household tasks such as
dishes, dusting, and picking up; an occasional party
with other young marrieds in their apartment complex.
Weekends they spent together, taking long walks in
the fall, ski trips in the winter, the beach or community
pool in the summer. So it went for three years.

Then their first baby, a boy, was born. A year and
a half later his little sister arrived. Suddenly, Carol's
life seemed to become quite complicated. With the birth
of their son she quit her job and took on by herself all
the domestic tasks of raising the children and keeping
the apartment. It wasn't that she didn't love her children
or want to be a mother, but Carol felt overwhelmed, so
tied down by the constant attention and care her growing
family required. She used to have a life outside her
home. She had enjoyed the adult companionship of
her business associates, the creative challenge of her
job at the agency. Now she barely had a moment to
herself, felt smothered by four walls. Carol was alone
all day with two active, growing children and with no
adult companionship from morning until night.

Carol began to resent the children for their never-ending demands on her time. She felt guilty, too, about her resentments because "good" mothers weren't supposed to feel that way, or so it seemed. Most of all she resented Greg because it was all so unfair. The children had changed Greg's life very little, but Carol's life had changed drastically. Overnight her role had been transformed from that of a highly successful career woman into that of indentured servant, nursemaid, cleaning lady, short-order cook, and live-in housekeeper.

Yet, Carol's transition to her new role might have been easier if Greg had understood her problem. Yes, he was willing to give the babies a bath and put them to bed. He'd even offer to help with the dishes — sometimes. But for Greg, such domestic tasks, after a long day in the office, were a chore, not a husband's duty. The last straw, as far as Carol was concerned, came at the end of a particularly bad day. She had asked him to pick up the rubble of toys and cookie crumbs, crayons and coloring books from the floor of their once-tidy living room. But Greg answered, with a laugh, "You can't watch television all day and expect to have a clean house!"

Carol greeted Greg's attempt at humor with pent-up rage. "I've made all the sacrifices," she screamed, "but you haven't done a damn thing but sit around and read the sports page! From now on you can see how much fun it is to keep house and play nursemaid because tomorrow I'm going back to work!" That evening, for the first time in their married life, Greg slept alone on the couch.

Carol did leave the next morning, not to find a job, but to see a lawyer. Fortunately, her lawyer, a close friend of the couple, sympathized with Carol's plight. He suggested, before they consider separation, that Carol and Greg honestly reevaluate their mutual roles, that they examine their feelings and attempt a fresh start.

The result of this reappraisal, after several weeks of honest give-and-take, was a written contract, witnessed by their lawyer friend, which outlined their mutual "rights and duties."

Carol still does the cooking, but Greg now pays a cleaning lady to help with the housework. Greg's "day off" is Saturday, Carol's is all day Sunday. Greg is responsible for the dishes and evening baths three nights a week, while Carol reads, does part-time public relations and takes a course in creative writing. At first, they followed their contract to the letter; now, they both know it by heart. Also, they trade "duties," and each is flexible enough to recognize exceptions. Recently, Carol canceled a class on an evening when Greg had to entertain an unexpected out-of-town client. Then Greg reciprocated with an afternoon off from the office the following day for a trip to the zoo with the children, while Carol went shopping with a friend.

INFORMAL AGREEMENTS

Family Court judges and marriage counselors have always advocated, as a therapeutic technique for troubled marriages, that couples draw up an informal agreement concerning conflict areas of marital behavior. The recent revival of interest in marriage contracts, however, has come from the Women's Movement. Feminist writer, Ms. Alix Kates Shulman, in *Redbook* magazine, shared with her readers the formal agreement that she and her husband drew up together as the basis for a mutual sharing of family responsibilities.[1] *Life* magazine found the idea so interesting — and so provocative — that it reprinted in a special issue on contemporary marriage, whole sections of the Shulman's 600-word document.[2]

1. Alix Shulman, "A Challenge to Every Marriage," *Redbook,* August, 1971, pp. 57, 138-142.
2. "Living by Contract," *Life,* April 28, 1972, pp. 42-46.

Today, unlike the past, some women are beginning
to see their domestic roles differently. They question
assigning household tasks merely on the basis of sex.
They believe, as does Ms. Shulman, that "husband and
wife should be responsible equally for their children
and household," that domestic duties and responsibilities
should be divided, "not according to sex, but according
to our personal needs, desires and circumstances."[3]
The rationale for such marital contracts is "equality
and self-determination."[4]

More subtle reasons may also prevail. Some young
couples, reflecting their own parents' sad failures and
the absence of a positive emotional climate to grow
up in, find it very difficult to trust anyone unconditionally.
They are torn between the feeling that marriage is a
trap and their very real needs for intimacy. So they
resolve this conflict by drawing up an ironclad contract
which is more like an "insurance policy" designed to
reduce the risk of failure to zero. Some of their statements appear more rigid and inflexible than the toughest
contract ever negotiated by the United Auto Workers!

Time magazine, borrowing the research of Dr.
Marvin B. Sussman at Case Western Reserve University,
recently quoted one typical example. "Ralph agrees
not to pick, nag or comment about Wanda's skin
blemishes. . . . Wanda will refrain from yelling about
undone chores until Sunday afternoon." Most significantly,
this particular couple also contracted not to use the
words "married to, married, husband, wife . . . and other
derogatory terms."[5] If they were not so tragic, Ralph and
Wanda's attempts at role-definition would be ludicrous.
Behind every clause in their contract stand two fearful
people trying to nail down their future with no risk of
failure—forever.

3. Alix Shulman, "A Challenge to Every Marriage," Pt. II, *Redbook,*
September 1972, p. 89.
4. *Ibid.,* p. 198.
5. "Ties That Bind," *Time,* September 1, 1975, p. 62.

The premarriage contract of Ralph and Wanda may also reflect, in a frightening way, the influence upon their relationship of the consumer-centered culture in which they live. People today are surrounded on all sides by price tags, from cut-rate cosmetics to the down payment on the latest car. Whether $1.98 or $19.95, everything today has its price. Popular television also reflects the climate of the times. Game shows are named "The Price Is Right," "Three for the Money," "Let's Make a Deal." We are all looking for the biggest discount, the best bargain. So we clip coupons before we shop and then buy more than we need merely on the basis of impulse.

Consumerism infects all aspects of our daily lives. The "price is right" mentality carries over even into our human relationships. Unconsciously, we price tag each other; we expect payment for our affections and for our services. All too frequently, we respond to others only if they pay the right price. We expect them to respond in a certain way, to bring to our relationship the correct amount of "change." Against this background of American consumerism, we can see why marriage would come to be described as a "50-50 proposition," or to be defined exclusively in terms of "rights and duties."

"Contract" is essentially an economic term. Unquestionably, it has proved very useful in helping all of us gain insight into our human relationships, especially the most intimate relationship possible between two people — marriage. Marriage counselors and popular authors have discussed at great length the various types of marriage contracts. They have described the psychological contract, the social contract, the different contracts for an "open" as opposed to a "closed" marriage. Yet, in a sense, every marriage does have its own contract, however informal or unstated, however hidden or secret.

Two people entering marriage always bring with

them certain assumptions, certain understandings about that relationship which concern mutual roles, expectations and social relationships. An explicit contract between a man and a woman describes in words what before was usually left unsaid. Used in this way, such a marital agreement can help a couple sort out their values, offer them a deeper insight into the dynamics of their relationship, help them to grow. Is it any wonder, then, given the fragility of contemporary marriage, the current interest in marriage contracts and their increasing use by couples as a means to help them define their roles and understand each other better?

Thus marriage, as a secular reality, becomes for many couples today a socioeconomic contract between two equal partners. But as a sacramental union between two Christians, can marriage be adequately understood solely by such terms? Ironically, that same age with its secular understanding of marriage as contractual "rights and duties," also has witnessed the development of a theological view of marriage in which the union is more richly described as a "covenant."

CONTEMPORARY CHRISTIAN UNDERSTANDING

The bishops of Vatican Council II, in writing their document, *The Church in the Modern World,* desired to define marriage in terms of a contemporary Christian understanding of the marital relationship. An early draft of their document attempted to speak of marriage in the old legalist language as a "contract," but this definition was rejected as too narrow and too limited a view of the marriage union. Instead, the Council chose to describe Christian marriage as an "intimate partnership of married life and love . . . rooted in the marriage covenant of irrevocable personal consent."[6] In using

6. *The Pastoral Constitution on the Church in the Modern World,* n. 48, *The Documents of Vatican II,* ed. by Walter Abbott, S.J. (New York: America Press, 1966).

the words "partnership" and "covenant," the bishops found a much deeper and a scripturally richer description of the two-in-one-flesh union of the Christian man and woman.

The concept of covenant has its origins in the unique promise made between God and the Jewish people; more than mere promise, covenant meant a special pact, a treaty, that described the unique I-Thou relationship of intimacy between Yahweh and his people. It implied that those who were committed to this union with Yahweh would abandon forever their lesser gods. Also, they would no longer rely on their own self-sufficiency now that they belonged to the One God upon whom all other forces in the universe depended. Yahweh, for his part of the bargain, would take the people of Israel as his very own.

Jewish literature attempted to describe this covenant relationship in many ways. It was like that of a shepherd and his sheep, the writers said, or that of a father and his beloved son. It was also compared to the tenderness of a mother for her child:

> Does a woman forget
>   her baby at her breast,
> Or fail to cherish the son
>   of her womb?
> "Yes, even if these forget,
>   I will never forget you,"
> Says the Lord almighty. (Is 49: 15)

But so deep, so special was Yahweh's love that it came to be pictured as most like the love between a man and a woman. Through the story of the prophet Hosea, for the first time in biblical literature, the unconditioned love of God for his own people was expressed in terms of marriage. Hosea, it seems, had taken as his wife a woman named Gomer. He loved her deeply, but

Gomer, after bearing two sons and a daughter, left her husband and her family for other lovers. It even appears that Gomer became a sacred prostitute in a fertility cult. Understandably, Hosea became jealous and angry. He wanted to abandon her forever. Yet, in spite of all that happened, Hosea found himself unable to cut the ties. He seemed to hear the Lord say to him: "Love her once again."

So Hosea resolved to follow after his wayward wife. The biblical author describes Hosea's feelings in this way:

> . . . I am going to lure her
> and lead her out of the wilderness
> and speak to her heart.
> . . . She will call me "my husband,"
> no longer will she call me "my Baal."
> . . . I will espouse you to me forever,
> espouse you with integrity and justice,
> with tenderness and love;
> I will espouse you to me with faithfulness. (Hos
> 2: 16-22)

No one knows the final outcome of the marriage between Hosea and his unfaithful wife, but Hosea, in these personal experiences, gained an insight into the love of Yahweh for Israel. In his struggles with Gomer, Hosea saw mirrored the Lord's relationship with his people — the fidelity, the forgiveness, the loving care of Yahweh for his covenant partners, the people of Israel.

Henri Nouwen has observed,

> Yahweh did not establish a contract with his people, but a covenant. A contract finishes when one of the partners does not adhere to his promises. Once a patient no longer pays his doctor, the doctor is free to prefer another patient instead; so, too, when a man does not keep his appointments with a psychologist, the

psychologist in turn does not feel obligated to
visit him and ask him why he did not come. . . .
In the covenant there is no condition put on
faithfulness. It is . . . unconditional commitment.[7]

Thus, Christian marriage uses as its model the ideal
of covenant — a completely different type of relationship
than a professional contract based upon reciprocity.
The foundation of Christian marriage is not an economic
relationship with the mutual monetary exchange of
"rights and duties," but a divine covenant which loves
without condition.

Here is the way theologian Monika Hellwig describes
the difference:

Covenant is different from a contract. In the
latter there is an exchange of pledges or commitments to quite specific obligations which
are spelled out beforehand so that each party
to the contract knows exactly what is involved
and what his responsibilities are. But in a covenant of alliance and friendship, the commitment
is open-ended. It is a pledge of personal loyalty
to be sustained in changing and unpredictable
circumstances. Marriage, therefore, is a covenant, because it is a total commitment of the
persons to each other. It is not to be con-
ditional on certain circumstances.[8]

To illustrate: Grant was a successful pediatrician;
Deidre, his attractive wife, a buyer for a fashionable
boutique. On the surface, their marriage seemed successful. At first, both could accept the fact that they
would probably never have any children of their own.
After several years, however, Deidre began to look in-

7. Henri J. M. Nouwen, *Creative Ministry* (Garden City: Doubleday,
1971), pp. 55-56. Reprinted by permission of publisher.
8. Monika Hellwig, *The Meaning of the Sacraments* (Dayton: Pflaum/
Standard, 1972), p. 72. By permission of Cebco Pflaum Division of
Standard Publishing.

ward and found herself wanting. She was, she felt, inadequate and barren, while Grant's life was productive. Deidre viewed their childless home as a personal failure; babies were proof of a woman's success just as a profession or a successful business were proof of a man's. By their 10th wedding anniversary, she was drinking heavily, often visiting a local cocktail lounge on the nights Grant would be late in coming home from the hospital.

One evening, Grant came home to find a silent house, a bedroom closet bare. On their bed was a note from Deidre. She was leaving to begin a new life in Denver with a bartender she had met in the lounge. "Please don't come after me," she wrote, "I can't stand the pain anymore." Grant first reacted in stunned silence, then with anger, finally with deep sorrow. The thought of Deidre in the arms of another man was, for him, too awful to bear. He had always been faithful, but she had broken their vows. Deidre had left him and their home for another lover. Close associates were surprised and sympathetic, but they urged Grant to obtain a quiet divorce. Rejected by Deidre, Grant, his friends felt, had every right now to rebuild his own life and begin anew.

The days passed, Grant's hurt began to ease, but the memories remained, memories of the way his heart had quickened the day he first met Deidre, memories of their first date, their growing intimacy, the night he had asked her to be his wife. Mostly, however, Grant remembered their wedding — the look in Deidre's eyes as they exchanged vows, his promise to her, "I, Grant, take you, Deidre, for better or for worse . . ." Grant had these memories, but he had feelings, too, feelings that somehow he had failed Deidre long before she had been unfaithful to him. Grant remembered, but mostly he understood that he still loved Deidre.

Some months later, Grant learned Deidre's new address and wrote a short note: "I don't understand why," he said, "but I do know that I was very blind. I still love you and I always will. If you ever need me, I will be waiting." He didn't expect an answer. No letter ever came. One year passed and then two. No word from Deidre. Grant went on with his practice and tried to forget. Then late one night, two and a half years after their separation, came a long-distance call. Deidre was crying; she had had a few drinks, perhaps, but she was still sober. "Grant, I need you," she said. "Please bring me back home." Grant left on the next plane.

The last few years haven't been easy for Grant and Deidre, but they talk more these days, understand each other's needs much better. Grant has cut back his practice; he is home now almost every night. Deidre has stopped drinking; she has come to accept herself as she is. The wounds have healed, the past has been forgotten; their marriage has become richer, their love for each other has grown much deeper. In the words of Ingmar Bergman, "They have walked through the vale of tears and made it rich in springs."

Secular reality or sacrament, contract or covenant — there is a real difference between the relationship of Grant and Deidre . . . and those marriages in which couples understand their union exclusively in terms of "rights and duties," roles and responsibilities. Carl Rogers sees that difference as the "dedication" which a husband and wife bring to their marriage:

> The commitment is individual, but the constant, difficult, risky work . . . is of necessity work that is done together. It recognizes that a relationship is lasting only if that lasting quality exists in the present moment. It makes no major attempt to clear up past or future difficulties, except as they make mutual life unhappy right now. It sees the relationship as a flowing stream, not a static structure which can be taken for granted. It focuses not so much on the individual, nor on oneself . . . but on the

immediate relationship which exists between the two. And so, occasionally, it achieves the transcendent quality which Buber describes so well . . . "The primary word *I-Thou* can only be spoken with the whole being . . . when *Thou* is spoken, the speaker has no thing for his object . . . He takes his stand in relation. . . . *Thou* has no bounds . . . No deception penetrates here; here is the cradle of the Real Life."[9]

Rogers concludes his understanding of marriage by saying that when dedication and commitment are understood in this manner, then "they constitute the cradle of which a real, related partnership can begin to grow."

This "dedication" to the ongoing relationship of marriage defined by Carl Rogers describes in secular terms the "loving fidelity" which an understanding of marriage as covenant adds to the contract concept of the marital union. Paul Palmer, S.J., has contrasted the difference between covenant and contract more precisely. A covenant is other-centered, whereas a contract, of its very nature, exists to protect personal rights. A covenant deals with persons; a contract is directed toward services. A covenant implies commitment; a contract states conditions. A covenant is forever; a contract can be terminated. A covenant is entered only by adults; a contract can be made by children. A covenant emphasizes the relationship; a contract stresses responsibilities. A covenant is an ideal toward which a couple strive their whole life long; a contract can be negotiated in a few days or hours.[10]

EVALUATING THE RELATIONSHIP

How do a man and woman determine, then, the relative value of contract or covenant in terms of their

9. Carl R. Rogers, *Becoming Partners.* Copyright © 1972 by Carl Rogers, pp. 201-202. Reprinted with the permission of Delacorte Press.
10. Paul F. Palmer, S.J., "Christian Marriage: Contract or Covenant?" *Theological Studies* 33, No. 4 (1972), 617-665.

own marriage relationship? It depends on several factors.

1. *For many couples, a written contract can represent a positive step in the growth of their marital relationship.* However inadequately or incompletely a couple may define their roles by such a contract, the very fact that they attempt to understand themselves in this way represents a sense of realism and a seriousness of purpose about their relationship that is refreshing.

For couples entering marriage, a contract can be the beginning of a deeper commitment to each other. It can serve as an excellent projective technique by which they are able to share together, before they take the final step, the expectations both bring to their marriage. Used in this way, a contract is a means of realistic testing for young couples who might otherwise enter marriage with unexamined values and unrealistic assumptions.

For couples already married, as in the case of Greg and Carol, a marriage contract helps define new roles and determine developing relational patterns. Role definitions that were once adequate may become outdated and outmoded with the passage of time. A written agreement, especially in a time of stress and crisis, can help a husband and a wife recognize those changes, face emerging responsibilities, and adjust to the new challenge of their marriage.

2. *For other couples, however, such a contract may represent a new form of an old legalism.* Wanda and Ralph, in their desire to avoid "derogatory" role definitions, may have merely replaced one rigid set of rules for another. This sort of contract can become nothing more than a trap leading to an adversary relationship. Rather than freeing Ralph and Wanda for growth, their agreement can become the cause of new arguments and endless bickerings.

Couples must always see marriage as a human relationship which requires for its success qualities such as freedom, spontaneity and mutual trust. In the best sense of the term, there are times when a couple should be able to "take each other for granted" in that they are able to count on certain things from their relationship, things like acceptance and understanding. An ironclad contract, or one too inflexibly applied, can create a "ground zero" situation where a man and a woman are forced to waste time and emotional energy proving themselves to each other over and over again.

3. *The ideal for Christian marriage is covenant, not contract.* The love of Grant for Deidre — and their story is real — suggests an alternative to the contemporary view of marriage as merely contract. There *is* a possibility of love stronger than death, "no limit to love's forbearance, to its trust, its hope, its power to endure" (1 Cor 13: 7). In a covenant, love implies fidelity, great maturity and lifelong commitment to the mystery of another person. From this perspective, a marriage understood solely as a contract appears, by contrast, shallow and one-dimensional. The climate of consumerism, the scars of deep emotional wounds, the fragility of the contemporary family may make it difficult, if not impossible, for some couples to realize this ideal of covenant. But to describe covenant as an ideal is not to say that it is unattainable for others; it is to affirm, rather, that marriage as covenant is a goal toward which couples can grow. It is the lifelong affirmation of the mutual "I do" spoken on the first day of their marriage.

On the first night of their marriage, Tobias expressed his relationship to his wife Sarah with this prayer:

> Blessed art thou, O God of our Fathers . . .
> Thou madest Adam and gavest him Eve his wife
> As a helper and support.
> From them the race of mankind has sprung.
> Thou didst say, "It is not good that the man

should be alone;
let us make a helper for him like himself."
And now, O Lord, I am not taking this sister of
mine
because of lust, but with sincerity. Grant that I
may find
mercy and may grow old together with her.
And she said with him "Amen."
Then they both went to sleep for the night.
(Tb 8: 5-9)

Marriage as covenant can be described in many
ways, "for better or for worse," "until death do us part,"
but never has it been expressed better than in the
simplicity of Tobias' prayer, ". . . that I may grow old
together with her."

Chapter 5
Is Our Marriage O.K.?

"What advice would you give someone meeting you for the first time?" asks the off-camera
interviewer. The slender blond woman on the
television screen fidgets nervously, "I guess
I'm too sensitive," she responds hesitantly. At
that, Jack, a utility-company technician watching the set, loses interest. "I don't think she's
my type," he says, "I tend to think she would
be looking for sympathy."[1]

Jack, sitting in the comfortable privacy of a dating
service office, is viewing a video-cassette "audition"
of Linda. Both are clients of a new kind of mate-match
that not only introduces couples by computer, but
enables singles to view prospective dates on videotape
before deciding whether they should meet. Video-
match may offer an alternative form of mate selection
for couples who feel uncomfortable doing the bar scene,
but a human relationship should surely promise something more than a one-dimensional view of a man or a
woman.

1. "Screening Process," *Newsweek,* May 10, 1976, p. 73.

So there should be a way for couples, dating or already married, to gain some insight into the directions and patterns of their relationship — not in the sense that men and women should "psyche" each other out, or be constantly analyzing their behavior, but from time to time it does help a person to step back, obtain a new perspective and discover the patterns of his life. Otherwise, people will make the same mistakes, repeat the same roles year after year and their lives will become little more than a succession of drab "instant replays."

Molly's marriage, for example, was an endless rerun of the same role. Her husband was a chronic alcoholic, literally drinking himself to death. After each domestic crisis, Molly would visit her sympathetic pastor for comfort and advice. "Don't you feel you've suffered enough?" the priest would question gently. Molly always nodded her head in agreement, but within a few days she would decide to "stick it out" one more time, she explained, "for the sake of the children."

Her husband finally died of cirrhosis of the liver. At the funeral, Molly's pastor breathed a sigh that at last her troubles were over. He was pleased, too, when Molly chose her second husband about a year later. Molly certainly deserved far better from life, the priest felt, than she had received until now.

A few months passed. Then, late one night, Molly knocked at the rectory door again. Her problem? The second husband was also a heavy drinker. Should she leave him or not, Molly wondered again through her tears; but after drying her eyes, she decided to give her new marriage one more try — "for the sake of the children."

Two alcoholic husbands elicit from their wife the same identical response. Is it random chance or a behavioral pattern? Family counselors and marital therapists, looking deeper, would see more in Molly's case than just coincidence. What are the relational patterns in a marriage? Why do some husbands and wives grow apart and others never seem to stop growing? When a man over 40 begins to feel restless, what has happened to marital intimacy? Why do some women become bored with husbands they once found so exciting? Why do the same arguments always recur, the same "disaster scenes" keep repeating?

Recently, some counselors, and some couples themselves, have begun to see in "Transactional Analysis — the 'I'm O.K., You're O.K.' " self-improvement technique— a new and exciting way to understand marital patterns and problems. The method aims at helping men and women discover the sources of their feelings and the way they usually relate to one another. Transactional Analysis (or T.A.) has been popularized in such books as *I'm O.K., You're O.K.* by Sacramento psychiatrist Dr. Thomas A. Harris and Dr. Eric Berne's, *The Games People Play.* One of the central goals of this psychological method is to induce feelings of worthiness, translated as being "O.K.," by releasing people from the "not O.K." feelings sometimes acquired during childhood.

The growing popularity of T.A. is due to its colloquial language and its emphasis on understanding human behavior as it reveals itself, not in the dark recesses of the past, but in present social situations or "transactions."

PERSONALITY PROFILE

The Three Faces of Eve, a book written some years ago and later a movie starring Joanne Woodward, described the real-life history of Eve White, a young southern housewife. Proper and shy, the quiet young woman had another side, another personality — a vulgar, one-night-stand, irresponsible identity that her doctor named "Eve Black." During the course of therapy, a third personality, "Jane," emerged. Jane was mature, adult, and well-balanced; eventually, this personality became the real Eve White.

The story of Eve White and her "three faces" is a very rare case in the history of psychiatry. T.A. theory suggests, however, that even the average personality is also made up of three easily identifiable psychological states. These three states are termed Parent, Adult, and Child (or P-A-C); and all of us — in our internal dialogues, as well as our dealings with each other — will always respond as one of these three "personalities," as a Parent, as an Adult or as a Child.

Everyday experience seems to confirm the presence of these three psychic states. There are times, for example, when all of us act very "Parent," even though we may have no children. A death in a friend's family makes us very comforting and we offer a shoulder to cry on. One of our business associates, or a student in class, fails to complete an assignment. We find ourselves pointing fingers, raising voices and threatening, "If I've told you once, I've told you a hundred times . . . !" Our bus is late, or the checkout line long at the super- market and we say with a sigh to the person next in line, "Isn't it awful — they really should do something about this!" Everybody, at one time or another, acts as a Parent.

Then there are days when everything goes wrong and we seem to take on the personality of a little child. We feel clumsy, make excuses, feel sorry for ourselves and are easily hurt by criticism; we may also just wish to avoid all responsibility and run away from it all, forever. A little child is in each one of us, too.

When we act "Adult" we live in the present, we make decisions on the basis of facts, and emotionally we react appropriately to situations. In terms of T.A. theory, the healthy personality is one in which the Adult deals with facts and maintains control, but indulges the Child (who is curious, finds life exciting, and likes to have fun) and resists the negative demands of the Parent (who keeps trying to offer outdated advice that tends to inhibit genuine emotional growth).

The most frequently used T.A. teaching-aid is a simple diagram of the personality:

P — Parent

A — Adult

C — Child

The Parent, Adult, and Child compare to two different tape recordings played simultaneously from two stereo-speakers. From one of the speakers, the Parent replays an endless tape of words inside the head — messages learned mostly from our real parents and still "heard" today. Some of these Parent messages were necessary; some were not.

This Parent voice likes to give advice: "honesty is the best policy," "look both ways before crossing the street," "never pet strange dogs," "birds of a feather flock together," "don't touch a hot stove," "little boys (girls) are seen but not heard," and so on. Many of our Parent tape recordings contain useful information that helps us through life. Some of the messages, however, are bossy, or foolish, or wrong. These kinds of Parent tapes should be ignored or erased completely.

At the same time these messages are being heard in the psyche, the Child "stereo-speaker" is also playing its own collection of tape recordings. Child tapes are not messages, but feelings — emotional reactions to persons and events in the past. These have an instant replay in the present whenever a person finds himself in a situation similar to a childhood scene of frustration and failure.

Doug, for instance, a construction worker, always

felt very clumsy and awkward when sitting in front of a desk in a private office. Even opening a new checking account made him feel small and stupid. His feelings had their origin in first grade when he was sent to the principal's office for misbehaving. Similar situations, even many years later, would trigger in him Child feelings first recorded during grade-school days.

In the middle of the personality diagram, between these two ego-states, is the Adult. This psychological position, according to T.A. theory, can have the same effect on the Parent and Child as a hi-fi tuner has on two stereo-speakers. The Adult, if allowed to function, can moderate the volume level of the Parent-Child tapes, maintain a proper balance between ego-states, and eliminate their unnecessary emotional static. Only then can he hear the real beauty of life's music — only then can a person live in the present as an Adult.

This does not mean that the Adult in us never pays any attention to the values handed down by his Parent; nor does it mean that we totally silence our Child, because feelings are a part of life. Certainly there are times when we should comfort or nurture like a parent; days when we need to be spontaneous, "break set," and escape the routine of life with the freedom of a six-year-old. The point of T.A. is precisely this: maturity means that one's ordinary behavioral patterns come from the Adult psychological state.

Transactional Analysis really becomes exciting, however, and offers a good starting point for self-understanding, when a person can recognize from which one of the P-A-C psychological states his own behavior flows. Basic T.A. texts — for example, *I'm O.K., You're O.K.* — list many common "clues" — words, facial mannerisms, and nonverbal behavior — that indicate whether we're living in our Parent, Adult, or Child states.[2]

2. Thomas A. Harris, M.D., *I'm O.K., You're O.K.* (New York: Harper & Row, Publishers, Inc., 1969), pp. 65-66.

The "horrified look," hands on hips, wrinkled brow, raised voice, pointing finger and clearing of throat can all be nonverbal signs of the presence of the Parent. Parent verbal expressions usually include words and phrases such as, "always," "never," "now you listen to me," "I'm only saying this for your own good," "now, remember," "if I were you . . . ," "if you ask me," "isn't it awful," "why don't you . . .?"

Child-state body language can be pouting, the "hurt look," whimpering, nervous giggling, quivering lips, foot stomping, tantrums, sudden tears, impatient interrupting and so on. Child word clues would include baby talk, "oh, wow," "nobody likes me," "I can't," "I won't," "I don't care," "I'm stupid," "Yes, but . . . ."

Everyone has an Adult ego-state and, with some rare exceptions, most people can live as Adult. The Adult in us maintains contact with reality, makes decisions on the basis of fact, runs reasonable risks, lives with ambiguity, calculates probability, and grows by experience. It takes inventory of the Parent, as one would clean a cluttered attic, accepts some messages, updates others, discards more. The Adult controls the noisy Child, restricts its undisciplined feelings, but, at the same time, leaves room for the Child's curiosity and excitement.

Dr. Harris lists some other Adult clues:

> . . . the basic vocabulary of the Adult consists of why, what, where, when, who and how. Other words are: how much, in what way, comparative, true, false, probable, possible, unknown, objective, I think, I see, it is my opinion, etc. These words all indicate Adult data processing. In the phrase, "it is my opinion," the opinion may be derived from the Parent, but the statement is Adult in that it is identified as an opinion and not as fact.[3]

3. *Ibid.*, pp. 67-68.

MARITAL RELATIONSHIPS

The P-A-C personality model also offers many insights into marriage relationships. T.A. makes it possible to understand — and even diagram — the different ways by which men and women respond to each other, the different levels of personality involved in the intimacy of a marital union. When we communicate, when we relate to another person verbally or nonverbally, we engage in what T.A. terms a transaction. The analysis of these interpersonal transactions is what the T.A. technique is all about.

Let's suppose that a married couple, Ray and Janet, are at a Saturday night party with some friends. Ray and Janet are genuinely enjoying each other's company; they are relaxed together and are sharing some laughs with the other couples. The transaction of Ray and Janet having fun together would involve both their Child ego-states. It would be diagrammed in this way:

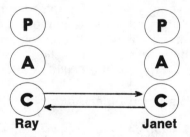

Later on in the evening, after they've both had their usual couple of drinks, Ray starts for the kitchen again, gesturing to Janet with his empty glass and asks, "Do you want another?" Janet, who is thinking of the late drive home, has now moved into her Parent state. She replies, "Don't you think you've had enough?" Ray is enjoying himself, however, is still in his Child state, so he responds, "Aw, I'll only have one more." Their transaction now looks like this:

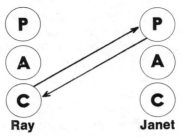

Ray   Janet

This is the classic Parent-Child transaction. Although Ray and Janet are in their mid-30's, the dialog is similar to that of a little boy asking his mother for another piece of cake, or if he can stay up to watch an extra half hour of television. It is also important to note that the lines of communication in the diagram of their transaction are parallel. T.A. language calls this a complimentary transaction. As long as Ray stays in his Child and Janet in her Parent state, communication will continue and the transaction isn't likely to cause any real trouble.

Let us suppose, however, that when Janet's Parent asks, "Don't you think you've had enough?" Ray shifts into his Adult state, evaluates the situation, makes a mature decision, and says, "I'll give you the car keys, besides we can sleep late in the morning." Ray's Adult response is addressed to Janet's Adult but if she isn't listening and stays in her Parent, then their interaction will look like this:

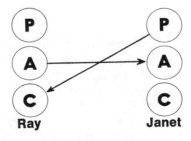

Ray   Janet

What has resulted here is a crossed transaction — the most frequent cause of misunderstandings in marriage, according to Eric Berne. In this type of situation, communication breaks down and is soon followed by negative feelings and frustrations.

Two people who are close to each other can transact as Child-Child one moment, Adult-Adult, or Parent-Child the next. What is important in a marriage relationship is not the incidental interactions that happen between a man and a woman, but the day-to-day, long-term, pattern of that relationship. Transactional Analysis can help couples understand their own ego-states and the habitual ways in which they usually relate to each other. It is extremely important that a husband and a wife understand each other's psychic roles in their transactions, because an open, growth-filled marriage can happen only in an Adult-Adult relationship.

Several common marital patterns deserve closer examination from the perspective of T.A. theory:

The Child-Child Marriage

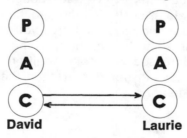

David, blond and ponytailed, met petite, doe-eyed Laurie at the local Day-care Center where they both worked as volunteers. College freshmen, they were attracted to each other from the very first day. Soon, friends saw them walking hand in hand across campus. David and Laurie shared similar interests — nature trails, small animals, and organic food. They were in love and the whole beautiful world was their playground.

David and Laurie were married their junior year and life was idyllic. Although a *summa cum laude* pre-med major, David decided to give up science and become a carpenter after graduation. He and Laurie built a little cabin, grew their own food, and opened a small crafts shop. Laurie's life was blissful, and so was David's — for a while. After a few years he was only moderately happy and began to feel vaguely restless. At 24, David decided to begin again the medical career he had abandoned earlier.

David now finds great satisfaction in medicine, but medical school has put a strain on his marriage and his relationship with Laurie. After a long day of physical examinations, clinical work, and study, David finds it hard to be interested in Laurie's world of plant care, handcrafts, and quilting. Recently, he has begun to compare her baby talk and collecting of stray kittens with the maturity and motivation of the women interns at the hospital. "You don't like me anymore," pouts Laurie, but as David has confided to a close friend, "It's not that I don't love Laurie — but I've grown as a person and she hasn't."

Their relationship would now diagram like this:

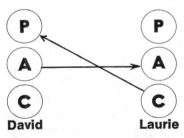

When a marriage is contracted by two Child ego-states, as it was by David and Laurie, important human differences are overlooked, realistic goals ignored, and expectations remain unexamined. Often, the Child-Child relationship is based upon superficial interests, such as "we both like music," "we both love animals," or, as in the case of David's and Laurie's marriage, "we're both into nature." Sometimes, this Child-bond is a form of protest against the world, parents, or the Establishment; it can also be an escape from life's realities and responsibilities.

Can this marriage be saved? Since growth is the first law of life, both partners must be able to grow together into their Adult states; otherwise, their transactions will become crossed and their marriage relationship will suffer severe, if not irreparable, damage. A marriage like that of David and Laurie may not survive the strain.

The Parent-Child Marriage

There are two common variants of this transaction: a. *Mother Parent and Little Boy Child* —

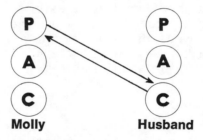

This diagram depicts the usual pattern of the relationship between Molly, mentioned earlier, and her two alcoholic husbands. The two men, both "loser" types, related to Molly from Child states that were dominated by feelings of worthlessness and self-pity. Their drinking set up a situation where the Child was severely scolded, not only by their internal Parent, but by the Parent figure in their marital relationship, Molly. "Can't you see what you're doing to me and the children?" she would say, thus reinforcing her husband's negative feelings in his Child state.

While the motivations of Molly's Parent are obviously complex, it would seem that her selection of two husbands with the same "not O.K. Child" would indicate the overwhelming influence of her own Parent and its need to nurture, to moralize, and to protect.

Sometimes, in group therapy, in individual counseling, or in the healing that only time can bring, it happens that one or another of the partners in this Parent-Child relationship will begin to function from the Adult. The transaction becomes crossed and a difficult period of adjustment then ensues.

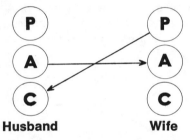

Husband   **Wife**

In this illustration, the husband has become a less passive partner in the marriage and has begun to assume an Adult role. Frequently, when this growth from Child to Adult occurs in the husband's ego-states, the wife will find it difficult relating to him in a new way, from her Adult. Nor is it unusual, after the first fight in their new roles, to hear her say, "I liked you better when you were drunk!"

b. *Father Parent and Little Girl Child*

The play *A Doll's House* by Henrik Ibsen is a literary masterpiece. It is the story of the marital relationship of a Norwegian couple, Nora and Torvald Helmer, and it is also the classic study of one woman's journey from psychological childhood to self-liberation:

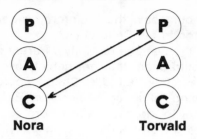

As the curtain rises, Nora tiptoes to her husband's door to see if he is in, takes a bag of sweets from her pocket, and eats them furtively like a naughty child. At play's end, when Torvald reminds Nora of her "sacred duties" to her husband and her children, and he says that before all else she is a wife and mother, Nora replies, "I have other duties just as sacred . . . duties to myself." Her relationship to her husband has changed:

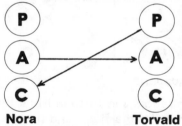

At the moment of liberation, the dramatic instant when the young wife abandons her Child role and begins to relate to her husband as an Adult, Nora says:

> . . . When I look back on it, it seems to me as if I had been living here like a poor woman — just from hand to mouth. I have existed merely to perform tricks for you, Torvald. But you would have it so. You and Papa have committed a great sin against me. It is your fault that I have made nothing of my life.[4]

4. Henrik Ibsen, *Four Great Plays by Ibsen* (New York: Bantam Books, Inc., 1959), p. 63. From "A Doll's House," tr. by R. Farquharson Sharp, in *A Doll's House, The Wild Duck, The Lady From the Sea.* An Everyman's Library Edition. Published in the United States by E. P. Dutton & Co., Inc., and reprinted with their permission.

Her husband accuses Nora of being ungrateful. Surely she has been happy in their home! Not happy, replies Nora, "No, only merry." She continues:

> . . . And you have always been so kind to me. But our home has been nothing but a playroom. I have been your doll-wife, just as at home I was papa's doll-child; and here the children have been my dolls. I thought it great fun when you played with me, just as they thought it great fun when I played with them. That is what our marriage has been, Torvald.[5]

Finally, it should be noted, not all choices toward liberation and self-fulfillment are necessarily made by the Adult. Sometimes, this apparently mature decision is actually a Child-choice. Joan Didion, the writer, has some interesting observations on some of the autobiographical literature of the Women's Movement:

> Eternal love, romance, fun. The Big Apple. These are relatively rare expectations in the arrangements of consenting adults, although not in those of children, and it wrenches the heart to read about these women in their brave new lives. An ex-wife and mother of three speaks of her plan "to play out my college girl's dream. I am going to New York to become this famous writer. Or this working writer. Failing that, I will get a job in publishing." She mentions a friend, another young woman who "had never had any other life than as a daughter or wife or mother" but who is "just discovering herself to be a gifted potter." To get a job in publishing, to be a gifted potter — bewilders the imagination. The astral discontent with actual lives, actual men, the denial of the real ambiguities and the real generative or malignant possibilities of adult sexual life, somehow touches beyond words.[6]

5. *Ibid.,* pp. 63-64.
6. Joan Didion, "The Women's Movement," *The New York Times Book Review,* July 30, 1972, p. 14. © 1972 The New York Times Company. Reprinted by permission.

Parent-Parent Transactions:

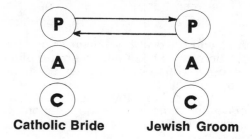

Dr. Harris has written that this type of transaction sometimes occurs between couples on the occasion of an interfaith marriage, when questions arise concerning the religious values to be shared with the children. Here is how he describes this type of Parent-Parent interaction:

> There are many cases where both partners have a strong Parent, but with different and frequently discordant content. Different religious and cultural content can produce serious difficulties if each partner feels the strong need to abide by the unexamined dictates of his Parent. Sometimes this difference is glossed over in the early stage of a marriage, only to emerge with fierce urgency with the arrival of children. Although a Jewish man may agree in advance that his children be raised in the Catholic faith according to the wishes of the Catholic bride-to-be, this does not mean that he may not be deeply troubled about it later on. The feeling here is that "my religion is better than yours" and, in fact, "our people are better than your people," which soon is reduced to "I am better than you." This is not to say that differences of this kind can't be resolved, but they require an emancipated Adult in each partner proceeding on an I'm O.K.-You're O.K. basis.[7]

7. Harris, *op. cit.*, p. 132.

T.A. AS A SOURCE OF MARITAL ENRICHMENT

A couple may be close physically and yet remain strangers all of their married life. Most husbands and wives sincerely want happiness for themselves and their families, but they become victims of patterns and behaviors seemingly beyond their power to change. Transactional Analysis provides a way out of this dilemma and creates opportunities for marital growth:

— *Individual persons, by using T.A. theory, can gain insight into their psychic states* and the causes of their present behavior. The "I'm O.K." technique also provides an easy language for men and women to express their deepest feelings and emotional reactions.

— *Couples are enabled to understand the kind of psychic "baggage" each has brought to their marriage.* A careful examination of the messages and feelings on their Parent and Child tapes will help a husband and wife discover much about the emotional basis of their relationship. For couples about to be married — especially if one of the parties has begun to have serious doubts about the soundness of the impending union — such an examination can be an enormous help in making the decision whether or not to proceed with the marriage.

— *The P-A-C personality diagram is a convenient way to visualize a couple's usual relational patterns.* Used along with the Parent and Child "clues," the diagram can assist both married and engaged couples in determining whether they relate as Parent-Child, Child-Child, or Adult-Adult. With marriage facing so many contemporary societal pressures, only an Adult-Adult transactional pattern can see a couple through the rough days of their relationship and assure continued growth for both themselves and their union.

— *Transactional Analysis provides an informal*

technique of self-counseling. With the difficulty, in some areas, of obtaining good marriage counseling and the great demand everywhere for therapists' time, T.A. techniques provide a "first-aid" approach to the normal stress and adjustments that every marriage faces from time to time. The book, *Born to Win,* by Murial James and Dorothy Jongeward, contains many excellent suggestions. For example, there are exercises that help explore the influence of both a husband's and a wife's Parent ego states in significant areas of marital life: money, possessions, fun, sex roles, listening patterns, work, values, parenting patterns and so on. How are we like our actual parents? What inner dialogue do we usually hear? What Parent messages have been incorporated into our own ego states? These are but a few of the many "do-it-yourself" T.A. techniques in the book that a couple can explore together.[8]

Transactional Analysis, with its clarity and insights, is an excellent therapeutic tool that can be used in many marital situations. Ultimately, people make good marriages, but T.A. can make better ones.

8. Murial James and Dorothy Jongeward, *Born to Win* (Reading, Mass.: Addison-Wesley Publishing Company, 1971), pp. 118-126.

Chapter 6
Free To Be You and Me!

The smiling couple look out at the camera from the deck of their new sailboat. Their clothes are mod; expensive binoculars hang from around the husband's neck. Beside them a picnic basket overflows with wine, cheese and long loaves of French bread. "Kids? Someday," reads the caption, and the ad for *Psychology Today* continues:

We both love children.
That's why we're not parents. Yet.
Because before we want children, we want to be ourselves.
To be Karen and Phil, before we're mommy and daddy.
The only responsibility we have right now is to be ourselves.
We're just as concerned about the world around us as we are about our own little world.
We'd sit down and write a letter to our Congressman for cleaner rivers, just as easily as we'd write a check for a new stereo, or a radar oven, or even scuba gear . . .
It's so much more fun to live your dreams, than to dream them.
Of course, we think about tomorrow. Who doesn't?
In fact, we feel secure about the future.
But today is where we live.

The goal of many men and women today is self-fulfillment. "I want to be me" say the lyrics of the familiar song and Marlo Thomas' children's book is titled, *Free to Be You and Me*. Self-fulfillment is such an important value in our society that some people assign it a higher priority than parenthood. There is even a National Organization for Non-Parents (N.O.N.), founded by Ellen Peck, author of the bestselling book, *The Baby Trap*.

Anne Taylor Fleming, in *Newsweek* magazine's "My Turn" column, wrote an article citing reasons for the conflict some liberated wives see between womanly self-fulfillment and motherhood. "Though we might in private moments yearn sometimes to trade back in our full heads and empty wombs for empty heads and full wombs," she said, "we cannot now."[1] Her article was answered a few weeks later in a letter to *Newsweek* by a doctor from the State of Washington:

> As an obstetrician-gynecologist whose office sees a daily parade of Anne Flemings, I have heard all the chic arguments against committed motherhood. It is of interest to me that Ms. Fleming left out two of the most common reasons I hear for the "empty wombs" she so ambivalently laments: (1) that pregnancy might disfigure the sexy bodies so necessary for American women nowadays, and (2) young American couples required to decide between the status of a Porsche and the dollar debit of a baby will opt for the Porsche.[2]

But is this put-down that simple? Is it an either/or proposition? Is the conflict between human growth and marital responsibilities that clear-cut? As long as feminine spokespersons see only two female conditions

1. Anne Taylor Fleming, "My Turn: Making Babies," *Newsweek*, Aug. 11, 1975, p. 13.
2. Russell Thomsen, M.D., "Letters," *Newsweek*, Sept. 1, 1975, p. 6.

possible — "full heads or empty wombs" — and other social commentators, observing Karen and Phil's priorities of stereo and scuba gear over parenthood, see it as either parenthood or selfishness, where are we? More important, where does it leave those women who try to be true to their growth as persons and yet feel responsible both to marriage and motherhood? They are trapped in a pressure cooker. On the one hand, religious conservatives say that a woman's place is in the home and expect her to cater to her husband and children, no matter what the cost to herself. On the other hand, her feminist sisters urge her to raise her consciousness, educate herself and begin a career, no matter what the cost to her husband and children. What factors have caused women to be squeezed in the vise of this dilemma?

FACTORS OF CHANGE

a. *History and Culture.* In the past, a man or his parents chose the woman he would marry on the basis of dowry, family, and utility. The peasant class paid close attention to a woman's health and fitness to work, much as one would select a farm animal. Upper-class women usually had two options — marriage or the convent. A woman's personal needs mattered hardly at all. Rarely did women have any choice as to whom they would marry. Marital happiness, in those days, did not mean love, but children and the performance of household duties.

Bishop Carroll T. Dozier has described woman's historical situation as a "long and subtle servitude."[3] And so it was. Society, for too long, relegated woman to an inferior role. Educationally neglected, sexually exploited, legally regarded as a "nonperson," the totality of her life could be best summed up in the German phrase as

3. Bishop Carrol T. Dozier, D.D., "Woman Intrepid and Loving," *Pastoral Letter to the People of the Diocese of Memphis,* Epiphany, 1975, p. 3.

"Kirche, Kuche, Kinder" — church, kitchen, children. At best, woman's role was that of an indentured servant; at worst, she was a slave whose whole reason for existence was to minister to the needs of men. Anatomy was destiny. Only in recent times has there been a long-delayed awakening. Bishop Dozier suggests two of many contemporary factors that brought about an enlightened awareness of woman's role in society:

> We had thought civil rights was an issue concerning black people, but . . . the civil rights protests revealed the personal and civil injustices that many deliberately and thoughtlessly imposed on others . . . women became career people and a large part of the work force of the country. They found employment, however, to be unequal, compensation to be unfair, hiring practices arbitrary, and advancement uncertain.[4]

b. *Roles.* Because of social and historical circumstances, but also because of her physiology, woman's role in society was thus severely limited. The French priest-psychologist, Ignace Lepp, in his book, *The Psychology of Loving,* has drawn the contrast between male and female social roles:

> For the majority of men, marriage is not an end in itself. They expect to find self-realization in professional, intellectual and political activities . . . Depending upon whether or not the marriage has been successful, it can be a help or a handicap to such activities, without their depending upon it entirely, however. Women look at the situation in a different light. It is true that they are conscious of their own personalities, and that they aspire to their individual happiness and self-realization. But the majority of them expect to find all these things in mar-

4. *Ibid.,* p. 2.

riage. . . . They look upon marriage not as a
means which affords them the opportunity of
living with the man they are in love with, but
as an end in itself. . . . This state of mind
undoubtedly is at the source of a great number
of disappointments in marriage on the part of
women who are no longer capable of being
"good wives" in the old-fashioned sense of the
term.[5]

Over 15 years ago, a priest hosted for a while a
weekly religious talk show over a local television station,
prime viewing time, 9:00 o'clock in the morning right
between "The Magic Toy Shop" and "Captain Kangaroo"!
Occasionally, the show would offer its viewers a free
"giveaway" — a holy card, a reprint of an article, or a
prayer. Usually, it would receive about 10 requests.
The priest was discouraged at first, but the station
manager assured him that this was a good response
since the most requests for recipes the station's cooking
show had ever received was five! One day a scheduled
interview canceled out, so the priest quickly wrote a
script on the role of the "Hard-pressed Housewife," which
was videotaped by one of the station's woman directors.
The religious commentator naively offered, as a giveaway to the program, a simple outline, "10 Steps to Be
a Better Housewife." Before the program was off the
air, the station's switchboard lit up like a Christmas
tree. The cards and letters began pouring in and within
three days the show had received over 400 letters asking
for the reprint. Some of the requests even came from
as far away as Canada. Many were long, anguished
four- and five-page letters describing the writers' failed
marriages, their sense of guilt, and their feelings of being
inadequate wives and mothers. In those days, the priest
attributed the incredible audience response to his
charisma as a television personality. Actually, he had

5. Ignace Lepp, *The Psychology of Loving,* translated by Bernard B.
Gilligan (New York: The New American Library, 1963), pp. 143-144.

touched a deep and sensitive nerve. Many women find living the traditional role of a "good wife" very difficult.

c. *Identity*. Helen Reddy sings, "I am woman, hear me roar . . ." and almost overnight the Women's Movement has its own "national anthem." The question of identity—especially sexual identity—has become a recurrent theme in American culture.

Several years back, a college paper began a column by an undergraduate feminist writer; its title was: "Ain't I a Woman?" Reading the young woman's views, week after week, one felt uneasy, almost embarrassed for the columnist, for it soon became obvious the weekly column was serving as sort of a psychic catharsis for the student author, a way of purging her own problems of identity. She described, in one lengthy story, how she had spent a whole day going through children's stores and "tot" shops, listing the types of clothing sold for little girls: slips, ribbons, panties, laces, frilly dresses. Then she told how her own mother had dressed her up this way as a child. The feminine role had been forced upon her, she moralized, and mothers were very wrong in forcing this same role upon their daughters.

Female *and* male identity is a human problem. At some time in our psychological development, all of us come to understand and accept ourselves as sexual beings. The reasons why this process of growth is delayed for some of us — and for others never really completed — are many: the demise of the extended family, the physical and psychological absence of many fathers, the lack of strong maternal and paternal role models.

For many men and women, the identity crisis, when finally resolved, occurs after many false and sometimes painful starts. There is something sad about a 38-year-old mother of three seeking escape and reassurance in a singles' bar; something pathetic in a middle-aged account executive still trying to make it with the "girls" in the office; and, yes, something tragic in a 10-years-ordained priest who is "great with the kids" but feels uncomfortable relating to adults, as an adult. Identity is a slow process.

"Make every day count, do what you really want to do, everyday, everyday, everyday" advises the Geritol jingle. Today, despite the locked doors of the past and the confusion of the present, women are becoming increasingly aware of themselves as persons. They desire for themselves all that being a person implies: fulfillment, freedom, and the right to happiness. If we believe that human growth is one of nature's first laws, that God reveals himself in the unfolding, forward movement of history, then, it would seem, we must also see woman's struggle toward self-fulfillment as a valid response to God's call.

A woman's response to this call is sometimes realized by the choice of a career outside the home. Or, it can be satisfied by a decision to find that fulfillment as a full-time wife and mother. In either event, the choice represents neither a passive acceptance of a social role, nor the quiet submission to cultural pressure, but follows the mature examination of all possible options. "The unexamined life is not worth living," said Socrates. Neither is the unexamined role of a woman in marriage.

But how does she find fulfillment as a woman *and* as a wife? It is just possible, of course, that any attempt to find a "middle way" is futile. Maybe Anne Fleming *is* right when she sees the choice to lie between "full heads and empty wombs." Perhaps Karen and Phil have chosen the better part. Perhaps. But novelist Anne Roiphe makes a telling observation:

> The very idea of removing by social surgery a woman's or a man's connected love for a child is part of a coming ice age of relation-ships — the dehumanizing of mankind. We may

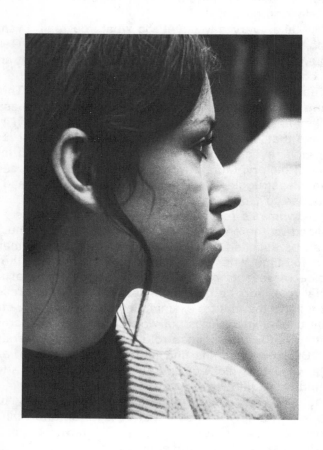

find that intellectual activity is not enough, that achievement in the industrial, technological world, while important, is not sufficient, and that we also, man and woman alike, need roots into biology, the touch of one another that childrearing brings. . . . As women, we have thought so little of ourselves that when the troops came to liberate us, we rushed into the streets, leaving our most valuable attributes behind as if they belonged to the enemy.[6]

A DELICATE BALANCE

Can a woman follow such a middle path? Is it possible to maintain a delicate balance between the demands of motherhood and her equally demanding urges for growth and fulfillment without losing herself or her family in the process? Feminist writers such as Caryl Rivers and Frances Ayvish answer yes, although they caution that there are no easy answers.

Since marital failures gain attention more often today than those marriages that succeed, it might be best to describe some of the positive factors that make the difficult balance possible. Several themes repeat themselves in the writings of those who have responded to the problem, not so much "10 Steps to Be a Better Wife," but the honest sharing of some landmarks on a woman's pilgrim journey toward a new and unfamiliar world:

1. *The Raising of Male Consciousness.* If a woman is to grow as a person and escape that "long and subtle servitude," then her husband must also gain fresh insights into her marriage role. One husband's letter has described this process very well:

My wife is a psychiatric social worker at a child-guidance clinic, and I am a teacher. We have a 12-year-old girl and an eight-year-old boy. We share the chores around the house as

6. "Women of the Year: Great Changes, New Chances, Tough Choices," *Time*, Jan. 5, 1976, p. 16.

much as any couple these days and I always felt that I did my share.

Late last summer my wife came down with a serious illness. During the six-week period she was bedridden and in the hospital, I cooked the meals, washed the dishes, tended to her needs, did the laundry, cleaned the house, and spent time with the kids when I had the strength.

For a while I got a kick out of the whole thing because I felt I was doing something valuable. However, after two weeks the routine became not only tiring but tiresome. I slowly began to realize how much I, as a man, was free from chores around the house and from the feeling of responsibility. I certainly did my part, but it was always in the spirit of "helping my wife," who, of course, had the major responsibilities. Now it was I who answered every call, whether it was for a late-night snack for the kids, or the fact that a wash had to be done.

I now feel very strongly that most men do not realize the burdens their wives . . . carry. We men are so used to being waited on, cooked for, and having our clothes washed that we don't even give the matter serious thought, other than "helping out." . . .[7]

Sometimes this new awareness comes very suddenly, as in the case of a wife's sickness or a husband's layoff from work. It can occur through a severe domestic crisis or, sadly, after the wife has left her home. Usually, however, to raise levels of consciousness, lines of communication must open between the man and wife, and that after a lot of mutual sharing.

But a man must also gain insight into himself, into his own role; he must feel comfortable with himself as a

7. Mel Scult, "Letters," *Ms.,* Dec. 1974, p. 4.

person. Extreme attitudes of male dominance can sometimes mask a deeper insecurity, which is terribly threatened by a wife who is no longer economically, educationally or socially passive. Shifting gears and relating in a new way to a woman who is different from the "sweet young thing" he married can be a wrenching experience for all but the most mature man.

Caryl Rivers has described how she and her husband were able to make this transition:

> . . . I felt more able to articulate my frustrations and he was able to understand that they were common to a great many women. He has been very considerate about trying to understand the things that were bugging me, to understand my need to be serious about my work, and I have tried not to get on a soapbox with movement speeches. We have the usual yelling matches now and then, but they are usually less intense than our disagreements over more cosmic issues, such as whether or not pouring the water from the dog's dish in the kitchen sink is a sanitary practice.[8]

2. *Self-discipline.* Mortification and asceticism may be out-of-style religious terms for "ordering priorities" and "setting goals," but the reality is the same. Growth in prayer or profession, social apostolate or social work comes only with a denial of one good for an affirmation of another. So it is with the vocation of marriage, as Frances Ayvish attests:

> Balancing both a career and a family is like walking a tightrope. I know, because I have done it these past 14 years, juggling jobs which have been absorbing and demanding against the needs, real and imagined, of my family. . . . Adjustments in home and family life are con-

8. Caryl Rivers, "Can a Woman Be Liberated and Married?" *The New York Times Magazine,* Nov. 2, 1975, p. 28. © 1975 by The New York Times Company. Reprinted by permission.

tinuous. It is not easy for husbands to lose the
constant availability and ego-support of a wife,
or for the children to understand why joining
the Brownies would add the straw that would
break the working mother's back, even if she
only works from 9 a.m. to 3 p.m. . . . The open
wound of divorce is dramatic, tragic and de-
structive. The day-by-day pain of self-denial
in a growing marriage is also searing, but basi-
cally constructive. Very few marriages in our
transitional world will escape one or the other.[9]

Self-discipline for many married men may mean
something as deceptively simple as an *equitable* sharing
of domestic tasks. "It's the same old baloney," one
wife told *Time* recently, "I come home so tired I can
hardly see and John flops down with the paper while I
stumble into the kitchen."[10] For other husbands, mortification may mean a refusal to follow the traditional
upwardly mobile success pattern, going on to "bigger"
jobs, in order that he may be present as a father to his
children.

For both husband and wife, self-denial means facing
responsibilities and sharing each other's lives. For some
this may involve a formal arrangement or a "contract";
for others, it may mean a simple "understanding"; for
all, it will mean self-sacrifice.

3. *Consumer Resistance.* Several years ago, a
theology instructor learned a lesson in contemporary
values. He needed some new texts for an adult religious
education class, but the cost would have been too
great for a slim budget. The theologian finally decided
to ask a fee of $10.00 from each participant. Registration
for such a course had been fairly good, about 30 students
a semester, but the instructor feared the new fee might
discourage participation. Yet the class registration

9. Frances Ayvish, "Where Are You Going, My Pretty Wife?" *U.S.
Catholic,* Oct. 1975, p. 39.
10. *Time, op. cit.,* p. 15.

more than doubled! Over 60 students had enrolled. Moral: people in a consumer society seem to make choices in terms of economics. If an object or a service bears an expensive price tag, however, then it appears to have greater value.

Jesuit theologian Father Walter J. Burghardt has observed that Women's Liberation cannot hinge simply on justice, on woman achieving economic equality. If liberation means only setting women loose on the job market, then their enslavement will merely transfer to a new locale. A woman in following a career can become as trapped in the economic market as much as a man in the ascending spiral of better job, higher salary, more consumer goods. After Karen and Phil's new sailboat, binoculars, stereo, radar oven, and scuba gear, what then? The real price, in the never-ending search for the elusive pot of gold that satisfies all consumer needs, is paid out one dollar at a time in our humanity.

As Frances Ayvish has observed:

> But I also detect a new pressure. "So and so's wife has done very well. She must be making about $15,000." Meaning, "Why aren't you?"
>
> . . . Much of the woman's movement is caught up in the drive for equal pay and status. And so it should be on a secular level. But as Christians we should turn this around and ask: "What are the most favorable conditions for me to use my talents in the world for the service of others? Do they include flexible working hours, enough money to pay household help adequately and to afford good supplemental child care, and enough status and authority to accomplish worthwhile goals?" By all means yes, and that may well include a five-figure salary. But the pay and status should not become ends in themselves.[11]

11. Ayvish, *op. cit.,* pp. 38-39.

Ends and means. Material possessions can become just as serious an obstacle in the path of human self-fulfillment as stereotyped sex-roles; both enslave. Jesus said we cannot love God and money. Of course, a family must use consumer goods, according to their needs and economic level, but it takes a sense of detachment for a husband and wife to use material things and yet not depend upon them. It takes — dare we use the term? — a *spirit of poverty* lest means become ends.

This is how Caryl Rivers describes how the struggle for self-fulfillment demands a constant sense of detachment:

> . . . I have learned a simple truth that I should have known: You can't have it all, all of the time. Many of the men of my generation thought they could, so they tied themselves to the conveyor belt, thinking that women would manage their emotions. They wound up with a vacuum where part of their lives should have been. My husband and I don't want that to happen to us. So perhaps I will not climb every mountain and ford every stream. . . .
>
> My husband will climb back on the merry-go-round but he will know when to get off. There will be areas in which we can't compete with the people who work 16 hours a day, who eat, live and breathe only for work. So be it.[12]

4. *Selfless Love.* The search for identity, growth and freedom is a response to God's call. But can it be something else? "We want to be ourselves, to be Karen and Phil before we're mommy and daddy," the couple say, and their words shadow a meaning that gives us pause. Does their hunger for self-fulfillment merely mask human selfishness?

As Father Burghardt observes:

12. Rivers, *op. cit.*, p. 31.

> The danger . . . is that *I* become the center of
> the universe. The way *I* see things, what *I* want
> and need, is what ultimately matters. And this
> is what makes for polarization. I do not care
> what *you* want, what *you* need; your vision of
> the universe, of reality — I couldn't care less.
> No, . . . the Christian context of liberation, the
> human context, is not *I* but the other: the Other
> with a large "O" and the other with a small
> "o" — the God who is my life, and the human
> person for whom I live.[13]

Selfless love or selfishness — discerning the difference is not easy. Human motivation is very complex,
very confusing at times, and all of us tend to be blind
in judging ourselves. Nor is it necessarily an either/
or proposition, all selflessness or all selfishness. A
surgeon once determined he would have the best lawn,
the greenest grass on the block. To him, weeds were
like cancer. So every day after coming home from his
office, and even before he had changed into his work
clothes, he would grab his tools and begin to attack the
crabgrass and clover that sprinkled his lawn. He never
learned what most of us amateur suburban landscapers
already knew; even with constant care, the best that
can be hoped for is more green grass than weeds.

So it takes a great honesty and openness and sharing with those who understand the patterns of our lives
to determine whether our personal search for self-
fulfillment is more "green grass or weeds." Always the
focus of our vision must be centered not on what we
are being freed *from* — for along that way lie alienation,
introversion and hostility. Rather, we should attempt to
discover what we are being freed *for* — because that
way leads to growth, to greater love and, especially, to
a commitment in the service of others. As Lutheran

13. Walter Burghardt, S.J., "Reconciliation in the Year of Woman:
From Theology to Action," paper delivered at the School Sisters
of Notre Dame Educational Conference, Baltimore, Md., Aug. 8,
1975, p. 7.

theologian Carl Braaten has wisely observed: "The quest for liberation not carefully guided by the demands of love in its multidimensional reality will only lead to new forms of alienation and oppression. . . . Women's power can bring justice, as it is doing in all fields, but only love can bring liberation."[14]

Ultimately, the point where one draws the line between legitimate self-fulfillment and the needs of those who depend upon us will never be resolved in a black or white way, or by recourse to popular psychology. It is a human problem that cannot be programmed or answered with a computer printout. In this case, perhaps only poetry can save us as we seek together to find our own "middle way":

> . . . let there be spaces in your togetherness,
> And let the winds of the heavens dance between you.
> Love one another, but make not a bond of love;
> Let it rather be a moving sea between the shores of your souls.
> Fill each other's cup but drink not from one cup.
> Give one another of your bread but eat not from the same loaf.
> Sing and dance together and be joyous,
> But let each one of you be alone,
> Even as the strings of a lute are alone though they quiver with the same music.
> Give your hearts, but not into each other's keeping.
> For only the hand of Life can contain your hearts
> And stand together yet not too near together;
> For the pillars of the temple stand apart,
> And the oak tree and the cypress grow not in each other's shadow.[15]

14. Carl Braaten, "Untimely Reflections on Women's Liberation," *Dialog* 10, 1971, p. 108.
15. Kahlil Gibran, *The Prophet* (New York: Knopf, 1961), p. 17. With permission of the publisher.

Chapter 7
Two's a Couple, Three's a Crowd?

Bill: Some of our friends, when we were still debating whether or not to have children, would point to the fact that there's overpopulation, that there's the possibility of some kind of nuclear holocaust before too long, and they'd ask, "Why bring a child into this environment?" And it wasn't easy for us to decide why. . . .

Joanne: In part, I don't think an adequate answer ever can be given verbally. But some of the reasons would apply more to meaning in life rather than simple happiness. I think children combine happiness and sorrow, they bring you both pain and joy . . . they are a way of finding another kind of meaning in life; not the *only* meaning, however, because then once they go you'd be an empty person. And that happens to a lot of people. . . .[1]

A young husband and wife, Bill and Joanne, were responding to an informal discussion among several couples on the topic, "Should We Have a Baby?" There

1. William J. Lanouette, " 'Should We have Kids?' " *The National Observer,* 10 April, 1976, p. 1.

was a time when most couples would hardly hesitate a moment before answering "yes" to that question. Today, some couples defer parenthood; others renounce it. According to Dr. Charles Westoff, Director of the Office of Population Research at Princeton University, 13 percent of married women aged 25 to 29 in 1960 were childless. By 1975, the percentage had risen to 21 percent.[2]

Other, less formal, indications show that parenthood is not prized as highly as before. For example, one college couple surprised their sociology prof by telling her that they were "V.C.'s" — voluntary childless. A *New York Times* headline warns, "Dad, the Endangered Species"; another feature article is titled: "The Case of the Vanishing Mommy." A future bride and groom compliment their Newman chaplain on a highly successful premarriage course, but then earnestly suggest, "You should have a workshop for those of us who are not planning on having any children." Choosing to raise a family used to be taken for granted; today such a choice is not necessarily a foregone conclusion.

MINDLESS MYTHS

What has brought about this change in attitude toward children and the family? Many factors are involved. One reason is that psychologists and social scientists have come to understand that some motivations for having children are a result of emotional insecurity rather than a mature choice to share human life and love. Insecure people can use children to prove their masculinity or femininity. A mother, for example, may want a little girl "doll" to dress up, play house with, or just to feel needed; a father may use a female child to satisfy his needs to nurture and protect, or use a little

2. Richard Flaste, "A Baby? Now or Later? Or Maybe Never?" *The New York Times,* May 7, 1976, p. B6.

boy as a way of achieving in sports what he was unable to achieve at an earlier age.

The reexamination of these and other "mindless motherhood myths," as they have been described by some feminists, is necessary and long overdue. But in exposing these myths — all real women want babies, families are always fulfilling, woman's place is only in the home — many positive parenting values have been forgotten or overlooked. In fact, just as "mindless myths" once propelled people into parenthood, so today, some couples avoid childbearing for equally unexamined reasons. One set of myths has been exploded, only to be replaced by new myths. Contemporary social commentators have described some of them as follows:

1. *The "Consumer Credit" Myth.* In a graduate education seminar at a large state university, secondary school teachers were once asked to describe their reasons for choosing a career in education. Some said they enjoyed working with young people; for others, it was the educational challenge. Finally, the moderator turned to a young woman who had sat silently throughout the whole discussion. "This may sound gross," asserted 25-year-old Amy, "but, very frankly, I teach so that with the extra income my husband and I can enjoy nice things in life — like redecorating our home and a new boat."

In a consumer culture, where everything has its price, people will indeed determine priorities in terms of money. In the past, children were an economic asset — the more children, the more breadwinners. A large family meant more helping hands for father on the farm; for mother, it meant more help around the house. Also, before the days of universal education, children were not economically dependent for as many years as they are today; they entered the job market earlier and were able to support themselves sooner.

Today, solely in economic terms, the decision to

raise a family means, if the wife is working outside the home after marriage, a reduction in the family income, other mouths to feed, children who will be economically dependent into young adulthood. The economic system, aside from an IRS deduction, does not encourage the raising of a family. Amy, therefore, can make a *conscious* decision to remain in the work force and not have a family because she assigns a higher priority to material things.

But what about those couples who become the *unconscious* victims of the economic system? James T. Burtchaell cites one typical example:

> A young woman at whose marriage I had offi-
> ciated came to me several months later to tell
> me that every night during intercourse she was
> seized with fear that she might conceive. They
> couldn't possibly, she cried, afford a baby yet.
> Knowing that her parents had given them a
> house and land, and that both husband and
> wife were working for good wages, I was rather
> surprised. As it turned out, they had gone
> heavily into debt to buy a $600 oak living-room
> suite, a $400 maple bedroom set, a $300 dining-
> room ensemble, $600 worth of kitchen appli-
> ances and $250 worth of laundry equipment.
> The unfortunate couple had been sold a bill of
> goods — not by the furniture salesman, but by
> the rotten and damned culture that had so per-
> suaded a man and his wife that a child came
> just below laundry equipment on their list of
> needs.[3]

2. *The "Fountain of Youth" Myth.* America, the argument goes, is a "child-centered" society. In terms of the decision to raise a family, this statement stands true, not in the sense that America is a society *for* children, but a society *of* children — perpetual children.

3. James T. Burtchaell, " 'Human Life' and Human Love," *Common-weal*, November 15, 1968, p. 251.

For many men and women in their chronological 20's, adolescence has yet to end. The teenage years have become an indeterminate length of time stretching from high school, through college, and beyond. Many elements in our culture reinforce the notion that it's all right for adolescents to remain kids forever. In medieval paintings children were drawn like miniature adults; but adults are depicted, in contemporary advertisements, as ageless adolescents.

Child themes — life as an endless summer, having fun, playing games — and child playthings — bikes, kites, beaches — keep reappearing in media promotions aimed at the young adult market. Notice the way Ron and Joan picture their Bermuda vacation in this magazine advertisement:

> We rode our horses along the surf,
> with the sun setting and the ocean slapping against the shore.
> It was a feeling of oneness with nature . . .
> We felt like children again,
> flying kites and playing in the surf together . . .

Garry Wills has described how difficult it is to mature in this sort of culture:

> Close to a decade is spent becoming a "kid" — all one's teens, and even earlier, the years we used to think of, loosely, as the time when people were becoming adults. It is a process costly and intense — the schools, the stereo, the bikes and cars and costumes. Then, blinking at the cutoff point somewhere in his early or middle twenties, the graduate is supposed to "un-kid" himself overnight, stop being what he has spent most of his remembered life trying to become. . . .

> How does one stop being a kid, when that was all one wanted to be?[4]

4. Garry Wills, "What? What? Are Young Americans Afraid to Have Kids?" *Esquire,* March, 1975, p. 170.

Children are not warmly welcomed at the banquet of life, for to have a child is to cease being a child oneself.

3. *The "Ecological Altruism" Myth.* Sondra and Gabe, like the couple suggesting a premarriage non-parents workshop, have decided to remain childless. Says Sondra, "I am a young professional and have very high aims in my career . . . that's going to be my 'gift' to the world." Gabe agrees: "There is overpopulation, already too many mouths to feed. It isn't right to bring another child into such an overcrowded world."

The overwhelming reality of world hunger and the inequitable distribution of the world's wealth haunt many concerned people today. Indeed, unlimited population growth and its consequent pollution are very real and very serious problems facing humankind. Some couples, like Sondra and Gabe, sincerely feel that the *only* legitimate ecological response is for them to remain childless. No one would challenge the sincerity of their conscience-decision, but some would question its validity.

The problem of overpopulation is complex. It has been popularized by concerned environmentalists — for example, by Paul Ehrlich in his book, *The Population Bomb.* Compare the opening page of *The Population Bomb* with a comparable passage in Dickens' *A Tale of Two Cities.* Ehrlich, in Delhi, India, describes the city swarming with its masses of people: people eating, people sleeping, people shouting, arguing, screaming; people crowding each other on buses, people begging, people living, breathing, dying; "people, people, people, people."[5]

Dickens, depicting prerevolutionary Paris, portrays essentially the same scene but with a different emphasis. For Dickens, it is hunger, not people, that stalks the land; hunger is written on the ragged clothes and city walls; hunger stares down from the smokeless chimneys

5. Paul R. Ehrlich, *The Population Bomb* (New York: Ballantine Books, Inc., 1968), p. 15.

and looks up from the filthy streets; hunger is the inscription on empty bakers' shelves and on every man and woman's face. . . .[6] For Charles Dickens, the problem is hunger; for Paul Ehrlich, the problem is people.

As a solution to overpopulation, a certain "lifeboat ethic" has been proposed. Extreme situations demand drastic remedies, some environmentalists say. If people are the problem, then reduce the number of people through Zero Population Growth; that is, people can reproduce themselves only once.

Other writers, however, disclaim the antipeople emphasis in some of the solutions offered by certain environmentalists. Richard Neuhaus, in his book, *In Defense of People,* puts it in this way:

> The person who is not a professional scientist is easily intimidated by those who are. What right, what unspeakable *chutzpah,* permits me, a religious thinker and layman in the mysteries of science, to challenge what all the scientists say about the population explosion? First, I share with the youth culture a deep suspicion of expertise in general and scientific expertise in particular. . . . Second, it takes only a little reading and consultation to learn that scientists are far from agreed on the nature and meaning of population growth. Third, the more passionate crusaders against population are intellectual litterbugs who leave strewn through their writings the wrappings of the political and ethical assumptions that inform their scientific conclusions. When I am told $E = mc^2$, I cannot argue, but when I am told $E - mc^2$ and means we should bomb Hiroshima, I have some very strong opinions.[7]

6. Charles Dickens, *A Tale of Two Cities* (New York: Harper & Brothers, 1958), p. 31.
7. Richard Neuhaus, *In Defense of People* (New York: The Macmillan Company, 1971), pp. 204-205.

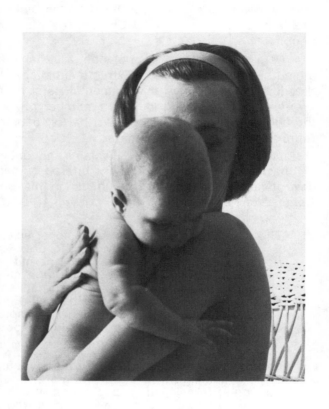

Idealism — concern for the world's problems — can be a beautiful commitment *to* people. Sometimes, as Michael Novak has pointed out, altruism can also serve as a protection *from* people:

> Sanity, we think, consists in centering upon the only self one has. Surrender self-control, surrender happiness. And so we keep the other out. We then maintain our belief in our unselfishness by laboring for "humanity" — for women, the oppressed, the Third World, or some other needy group. The solitary self needs distant collectivities to witness to its altruism. It has a passionate need to love humankind. It cannot give itself to a spouse or children.[8]

RESPONSIBLE PARENTHOOD

The problem for most husbands and wives today, however, is not *whether* they should have children, but *how many* children and *how soon?* How *does* a couple decide?

Loraine and Bob have been married for 10 months and have been living in San Francisco where Bob works as a radio announcer on a small station and Loraine is a nurse. They come back East to spend a few days of their summer vacation with Loraine's parents in Cincinnati. One evening, as they are doing the dishes together, Loraine's mother says, half with a smile, half with a question, "I suppose any day now I'll hear I'm going to be a grandmother." "Mom," responds Loraine firmly, "Bob and I have decided to wait a couple of years, until we're both ready, before starting a family." "Well, I just don't understand you young people," snorts her mother. "In my day we didn't *plan* anything. We knew God wouldn't send us any more children than we

8. Michael Novak, "The Family Out of Favor," *Harper's,* April, 1976, pp. 39-40.

were able to take care of!"

It is easy to understand, even up until Loraine's mother's generation, how parents would passively accept "all the children that God will send." Social and religious reasons supported this uncomplicated understanding of parenthood: infant mortality was high; woman's role was limited; popular preaching and piety did not give sufficient attention to freedom of conscience and human responsibility. Some couples, trying very hard to live up to the large-family ideal, succeeded in raising many children; other husbands and wives found parenting very difficult, and as a result their marital relationships and family life suffered.

Vatican Council II, recognizing the new historical and social complexities of marriage and the stresses imposed by the demands of modern life, put to rest forever, so far as Catholics were concerned, the "bigger the family, the better" myth. The Council spoke about responsible parenthood and addressed the situation of couples like Bob and Loraine:

> For in view of the inalienable human right to marry and beget children, the question of how many children should be born belongs to the honest judgment of the parents.[9]

The Council also affirmed:

> The parents themselves should ultimately make this judgment in the sight of God. But in their manner of acting, spouses should be aware that they cannot proceed arbitrarily.[10]

How does a couple make a clear choice about having children? How do they sort out the good reasons

9. *The Pastoral Constitution on the Church in the Modern World,* n. 87, *The Documents of Vatican II,* ed. by Walter Abbott, S.J. © 1966 by America Press, 106 W. 56 Street, N.Y. 10019. All rights reserved.
10. *Ibid.,* no. 50.

from the wrong ones for postponing pregnancy? Just as a tennis player, in a Virginia Slims tournament, does not decide for herself an opponent's bad serve, but waits for the line judge to cry "Fault!" so there should be objective ways for a couple to measure motives. The human heart is very fickle; there is always great possibility for self-deception. Decisions to have or not to have children can both be made "arbitrarily" on the basis of self-centeredness and selfishness.

So the Council advises, as a general rule, that sincerity and good intentions alone are not enough. It suggests several criteria or guidelines by which a husband and a wife can assure that their motives for responsible parenthood remain unselfish and within the context of truly human love.[11] These criteria might be formulated as three questions: "What are our capabilities? What are our possibilities? What of our love in light of the gospel?"

1. *What are our capabilities?* In answering this question, a husband and wife should take into consideration their own health and age, physical and psychic strength, and their present and future financial situation.

Loraine and Bob, for example, made their decision to postpone a family for a few years on the basis of their answer to this question. While they both want a child very much, both are repaying state and federal college loans. Bob is paying back almost $8,000; Loraine owes about $5,000. In view of Bob's modest starting salary in radio and their heavy debts, it is the honest judgment of Bob and Loraine that a pregnancy this soon in their marriage, and Loraine unable to work, would cause an intolerable financial strain.

Age can sometimes be a factor in making this decision. Edward, a laicized priest in his mid-40's, has recently married Pat, a lawyer, who is about 34 years old.

11. *Ibid.,* no. 51.

Both Edward and Pat want a family, but Edward is concerned that he will be in his 60's — grandparent age — when his children are in high school. Pat wonders about the risks of childbirth. After giving the matter serious thought, Edward and Pat elected to have a family. Edward reflected that longevity was a characteristic trait in his family — both his grandparents had survived until their late 80's and his own parents were very active in their retirement years, looking and acting as alert and alive as a couple in their 40's. Pat's doctor admitted frankly that childbirth was much easier for a younger woman, but also said that the risks were not that high and there was a relative lack of danger in pregnancy even for a woman in her late 30's or early 40's. Edward and Pat realize that their decision might not be that decision of many couples in their situation, but they both felt, all factors considered, that they have made the right decision for themselves.

Psychological Factors should also be taken into consideration. As John J. and Mary Perkins Ryan observe in their book, *Love and Sexuality:*

> . . . people vary enormously in their capabilities to handle children. Some fortunate couples can raise a large family and manage to have love and joy predominate over the stresses and strains. Others, with different temperaments and capabilities, find themselves almost dehumanized by the care of two or three children; they feel lost in a fog of weariness and uncongenial occupations. Until good child-care centers and help with the household are more generally available (and even if they were, for some couples), having a large family will often not be the most generous decision; there will be many cases where the care of several children would make loving almost impossible.[12]

12. Mary Perkins Ryan and John Julian Ryan, *Love and Sexuality* (Garden City: Doubleday Image, 1969), p. 160. Copyright © 1967 by Mary Perkins Ryan and John Julian Ryan. Reprinted by permission of Holt, Rinehart and Winston, Publishers.

2. *What are our possibilities?* What effect, if any, will the raising of a family have on the particular paths that lie open to a husband and a wife? What opportunities for individual growth and enrichment are available to the couple as persons? Is there a special contribution a husband and a wife can make to the well-being and enrichment of their community?

In the case of individual growth, ways to maintain the delicate balance between personal self-fulfillment and family life have already been suggested in the chapter, "Free to Be You and Me!" But what about creative talents necessary for the welfare of society? Is it not possible that a husband or a wife might discover that certain skills and abilities — artistic, literary, scientific or medical — could not flourish within the context of an active, demanding family life?

To illustrate: Carter and Sylvia are a husband and wife medical team. Both are physicians, their field of specialization is the treatment and cure of cancer. Sylvia is a highly skilled surgeon; Carter, a specialist in chemotherapy. Their marriage greatly enriches their professional relationship and mutual interests. As a result, many lives have been saved and suffering people offered hope by this couple's healing hands and great professional skills. What are the family "possibilities" for Sylvia and Carter? The Ryans, commenting on just such a case, make this observation:

> The question even arises: might not a particularly talented and trained couple — two doctors, for instance — who are making some special contribution to society through their work, when this work is of such a demanding and absorbing nature that they could not give children the attention they should have, plan to get married and not have any children at all? . . . Might not some couples who are physically capable of producing children, therefore, be entitled to refrain from doing so if try-

ing to bring up children would seriously inter-
fere with their making a particular contribution
to society?[13]

3. *What of our love in light of the gospels?* Jesus
once said, "Where your treasure is, there will your heart
be also" (Mt 6: 21). The value a couple sees in raising
a family will depend upon what their hearts prize as
the goals of their marriage, the particular meaning they
find in married life. In considering parenthood, in weigh-
ing all the popular articles and arguments for and against
a family, a married couple really comes to grips with
two contrary views of human nature current in society
today — the secular humanist view and the Christian
view. The emphasis, in the humanist view of man, would
be on self-fulfillment, *independence,* where one would
assert, "I am." The Christian view, on the other hand,
assigns a higher value to *interdependence.* While it
also affirms, "I am . . . ," it adds immediately afterwards,
"my brother's keeper." Differing value systems thus
result in different choices.

The central focus of a humanist view of marriage,
as stated in a book such as *Open Marriage,* would be on
personal fulfillment, individual enrichment. The open
marriage view does not, of course, discourage children
and family, but accepts them only to the degree that
they enhance human growth goals, only as long as they
help people become all that they are capable of
becoming.

The Christian perspective is different. While accept-
ing growth as one of nature's primary laws and recognizing the vital importance of self-fulfillment, those who
follow the teachings of Jesus would assign an even
higher priority to self-surrendering love. "A man can
have no greater love than to lay down his life for his
friends" (Jn 15: 13). Marriage is thus viewed by Chris-

13. *Ibid.,* p. 161.

tians as a union of love in the service of life — always open to growth, but the kind of growth that fundamentally defines itself in relationship to another. Rather than measure the value of family life in terms of rigidly predetermined goals of personal growth, the Christian view would measure self-fulfillment and human growth in terms of marriage and the family.

Here is the way it happened in the life of one couple: Monica and Lance later described it as the longest day of their lives. The doctor had spoken first to Lance, soon after the birth of their second child, Sheila, a beautiful baby girl. The doctor said only that he was concerned, but that he wanted a pediatrician to examine Sheila to be sure, before breaking the news to Monica. After the tests were completed, the moment came that neither Monica nor Lance would ever forget — they were told that Sheila was an exceptional child.

"We had our married life all mapped out before us," said Monica, a legal secretary. "We planned everything exactly the way it would be. I'd work for a couple of years, then take time off to have our two children. We figured it was better to have them close together for companionship. Then, when they were old enough, there was a nearby day-care center, and I'd go back to work full-time. The only thing we hadn't figured on was Sheila's brain damage. Learning that news was our 'longest day.' "

Lance comments: "It's hard to describe now the way we felt then — shock, resentment, 'what have we ever done to deserve this?' — those kinds of feelings. Our world was turned upside down, all our carefully laid plans ruined — or so we thought. . . ."

"What seemed to be our worst day," added Monica, "turned out, instead, to be the richest moment of our lives." Lance nodded agreement. "I had to make a choice," Monica continued. "Either send Sheila away or quit work, stay home, and with Lance's help, take care of her myself. It seemed like such a big sacrifice at the time, but Sheila's presence has made us both grow in ways we never expected or planned. We're closer as a couple. Things we used to want out of life don't seem that important now."

"We were not really that religious," concluded Monica, "but we've come to realize that our beautiful little girl is the best gift God ever gave us. Through her we've come to see how selfish we really were when we thought we had our whole lives planned down to the last detail. Sheila has called out of our hearts a power to love we never knew was there, never dreamed possible. We don't know how many more years God will leave her with us, but we live day by day, grateful for every moment."

Self-surrendering love is not the same as a martyr complex, not the glib "offer it up" attitude that sometimes masks cheap religious piety. Nor is this love possible, except for those who have a strong sense of self-worth and have come to terms with their own identities as persons and as Christians. It is a free, unselfish gift of oneself to another, using as a model the life and example of Jesus Christ.

Finally, when considering responsible parenthood, a couple must also examine the moral or ethical dimension of family planning *methods*. Married persons, who have made a responsible choice that they should postpone a pregnancy, sometimes feel trapped in a dilemma. They feel the very human need to express and deepen their love through sexual intercourse, but they are also aware of traditional Catholic teaching that frowns on certain methods of family planning. God seems to be saying one thing in their hearts and another thing through his Church.

What should a couple do? Perhaps the best response to that question is found in the most widely read Catholic marriage preparation manual in use today.

The book, *Together for Life,* and its author, Msgr. Joseph M. Champlin, respond to the dilemma with these words:

> There is no easy resolution of that issue, but neither does God want couples to be terrified every time they make love. In the complexities of life all of us on occasion become similarly torn between conflicting commands. At those times we purify our hearts, search for God's light in this special circumstance, then decide what is the best course to follow. And follow it without fear or anxiety.[14]

WHY BE A PARENT?

Joanne, in trying to share some of the values she experienced in parenting, said it best of all: "I don't think an adequate answer can ever be given verbally. But some of the reasons would apply more to meaning in life rather than in simple happiness." The positive values of parenthood, the reasons why a husband and a wife make a conscious choice to raise a family, are more "meanings" they discover together rather than the result of cold logic. This is the way, for example, that Joanne describes a refreshing new dimension of life that came about with the birth of her daughter, Nicole:

> . . . one of the joys that I could never anticipate is just seeing her wake up in the morning and smile. When she gets up on her arms, and looks up, and looks at you, and smiles. I have never known — and I love Bill very much — but I have never known another kind of love. And I love Nicole in ways that I have never loved other people before. And that love wasn't there before. It grew.[15]

Hard, really, to give "reasons" for parenthood. But

14. Joseph M. Champlin, *Together for Life* (Notre Dame: Ave Maria Press, 1975), p. 61.
15. Lanouette, *op. cit.,* p. 14.

it would be dishonest to write only of the difficulties of the family, and not of its beauties. Out of the many special pleasures of parenting, it is possible to describe just a few of its many meanings:

Parenthood is the creation of another person. It is the pleasure of creating with one's beloved a new human personality, a new person with his own unique identity, different, in some marvelous way, from every human being that has ever lived, living today, or yet to be born.

Several years ago, *Life* magazine in an article about the birth of a woman's first baby, described the wonder of creation with these words:

> Whatever feelings pregnancy may arouse — delight, indifference, resignation, horror — the very idea of creating a new human being is awesome. Pregnancy is surely the most creative thing you will ever do — even if you have done it inadvertently. And the process itself is miraculous — so hard to believe that at an already appointed hour you will divide like some ancient cell, and suddenly it won't be just you any longer but you and some other being, to whom you will be tied, by nerves and tissue and chemistry, all your life. This being is already within you, shouting in a sometimes deafening voice, look out, stand back, here comes a whole new person. And you are the lifeline, its substance, its nourishment. Only you can make sure that its bones are strong and its eyes are clear. How good you must be, how well behaved, how faithful to this being.[16]

Parenthood enriches a marital relationship. Vatican Council II put it this way in theological language:

> Marriage and conjugal love are by their nature ordained toward the begetting and educating of children. Children are really the supreme

16. Eleanor Greaves, "A Woman on Her Way to a Miracle," *Life,* July 22, 1966, p. 48. Copyright © 1966 Time Inc.

gift of marriage and contribute very substantially to the welfare of their parents.[17]

How, some people would ask after hearing those words, can the Church dare describe children as the "supreme gift of marriage" when they tie you down, interrupt your conversations, take away from your privacy, empty your bank account, exhaust your body, shatter your nerves, and tear apart your beautiful home? How can children be said to enhance a marriage when all they seem to bring is more problems? Judith Viorst, a writer who is also a wife and a mother, responds in this way:

> I don't deny that this may be the truth for many marriages, but it isn't the truth for the marriages I know. For most of the women I've talked to, including myself, believe that children *add* to the pleasures of marriage in spite of the messes and stresses and strains and restrictions and expenses that accompany them. Why? Because if shared experiences like travel or bowling or Bach or playing cards or fishing or collecting antiques can help to bind a marriage closer together, then surely a child, who binds us together in so many different ways — emotionally, biologically, historically — has to be the ultimate shared experience.[18]

Parenthood is the gift of our own personalities. More than even the awesome creation of new physical life, a mother and a father are also able to pass on to their children their own unique identities, interests, and values. These may be some simple pleasures that they both love and enjoy — drawing or baking or telling stories or just knowing how to build a bookcase; they may be creative talents like art or music or poetry; it may be

17. *Op. cit.,* no. 50.
18. Judith Viorst, "Kids!" *Redbook,* June, 1976, p. 144. Copyright © 1976 by Judith Viorst.

that parents are able to extend themselves onward toward people yet to be born and with them an undreamed of richness of life that will only blossom to beauty two or three generations later.

Sean, second-generation Irish and already well established in a professional career, began writing seriously when he was in his 40's. First, he wrote for his own amusement and then, at the urging of friends, for publication — poems, articles and, finally, several books. Sean couldn't put his finger on the exact moment his literary skills had begun to develop, but he was sure he knew when the seed was planted.

Sean remembered, when he was a little boy of eight and confined to bed for over a year, how his mother had read out loud to him almost every afternoon — the poetry of Rudyard Kipling and Robert Louis Stevenson's, *A Child's Garden of Verses.* At an even earlier age, when he was four or five, Sean used to climb into his dad's lap every evening after supper. Although his father was a busy member of the medical profession, with extraordinary demands upon his time, the doctor would always have time for his little boy. He would put down the evening paper, and with small Sean nestled in his arms, begin reading stories of the great heroes of American history — Miles Standish and the Plymouth Colony, Betsy Ross and the first flag, Patrick Henry before the Virginia House of Burgesses.

Sean knew his parents had shared their own rich heritage — a love of language and a way with words; he now understood, in those very special moments together, that his mother and father had given him something worth much more — their love and a sense of his own identity as a person.

Is three a crowd? Hardly ever, or as Michael Novak has so beautifully described it:

To marry, to have children, is to make a political

statement hostile to what passes as "liberation" today. It is a statement of flesh, intelligence, and courage. It draws its strength from nature, from tradition, and from the future. Apart from millions of decisions by couples of realistic love, to bring forth children they will nourish, teach, and launch against the void, the human race has no future — no wisdom, no advance, no community, no grace . . .

It is the destiny of flesh and blood to be familial.[19]

19. Novak, *op. cit.*, p. 46.

Chapter 8
What Is This Thing Called Love?

Recently, in a large Midwestern city, the daughter of a prominent Mafia family was married. The music played at the wedding was, of course, "The Theme from the Godfather." Many different melodies are heard at weddings today, songs that have a personal meaning for the new bride and groom. "We've Only Just Begun" and "The Two of Us" by the Carpenters are two contemporary favorites. Less frequently heard, but still special to some couples are: "Follow Me," "Lara's Theme" and "I Know I'll Never Find Another You." Many more couples have found Paul Stookey's "Wedding Song" especially appropriate:

> Well then, what's to be the reason
> for becoming man and wife?
> Is it love that brings you here,
> or love that brings you life?
> For if loving is the answer
> Then who's the giving for?
> Do you believe in something
> That you've never seen before?
> O, there's love, there's love.[1]

1. Paul Stookey, "Wedding Song" (New York: Public Domain Foundation, Inc. 1971). All rights reserved. Used by permission of Warner Bros. Music.

We sing of love at weddings, pine for love when parted, share tender words of love together. But what is this thing called *love?* Songwriters tell us "All You Need Is Love"; poets say "love's a sickness full of woes," " 'tis what I feel, but can't define, 'tis what I know, but can't express"; psychologists, recognizing that "you're nobody, 'til somebody loves you," describe adulthood and emotional maturity as the ability to accept and return love. Theologians picture heaven as love, possessed forever, and describe hell as a long and terrible loneliness — the complete and total absence of love.

Jesus, when once asked to sum up the meaning of life, answered in terms of love — love of God and love of neighbor. He forgave a sinful woman because, as he described it, "she has loved much." He was betrayed by his friend, Peter; yet when they met later, Jesus asked only one question of Peter for his forgiveness, but he asked it three times: "Peter, do you love me?" Finally, Jesus told his first followers, "Love one another as I have loved you" (Jn 15: 12) and said that people would recognize them as his friends by the love they had for one another.

What *is* love? A coed comes back from a date and tells her roommate, "I think I'm in love," a 40-year-old man whispers for the first time, "I love you," a teenage couple announce to a happy family, "We're in love!" What does that word, "love," mean? What *is* love?

There are almost as many descriptions of love as there are lips to give them utterance. Love is so personal, such a unique, yet universal human experience, that there are as many meanings of love as there are lovers. Part of the problem is in the words used to describe love. The English language, at least in everyday conversation, lacks sufficient words to describe the complex realities we mean when we say, "I love you." English has one word, other languages, many. Greek words like *eros, philia, agape* depict different aspects, different realities which we group together with the single English word: "love."

Just as a traveler in a foreign country carries along a phrase book to understand an unfamiliar language, so too, it is important for us to have some handy guide or framework to help us sort out for ourselves the different levels of meaning when one person says to another, "I love you." Fortunately, there are many excellent "traveler's guides" to love. Almost every modern social scientist and psychologist has his own way of describing the "many-splendored" levels of love. Erich Erickson, Abraham Maslow, Victor Frankl, Erich Fromm — each has shared his own unique understanding of love's many meanings. We should use the description that suits us best.

THE ANATOMY OF LOVING

One of the easiest methods to sort for ourselves the different ways of loving is to think of love as existing on three levels of meaning — physical, psychological, and spiritual. In turn, we will take each expression of love and comment briefly on some of the implications each holds for modern marriage:

Physical — The word we use to describe the physical love union between a man and a woman is *sex.* Today, when a couple exchange vows they say: "I, Brad, take you, Kathy, . . ." But the marriage formula used by Catholic couples in England before the Reformation was much more honest, much more expressive of the sexual side of love. Couples in those days would say, "With this ring I thee wed, and with my body I thee worship. . . ."[2]

2. Paul F. Palmer, S.J., "Shall They Make a Covenant?" *The Priest,* July-August 1975, p. 16.

Victorian prudery tried to pretend that a married couple could have love without sex. Today, some couples would reverse that and say they can have sex without love. For example, in the Dustin Hoffman-Mia Farrow movie, *John and Mary,* a man and a woman pick each other up one Friday night in a singles' bar. They spend the weekend having sex. Monday morning arrives and as they leave to go their separate ways, the man introduces himself, "I'm John." The woman replies, "My name is Mary."

The tendency in our times to separate sex from love may be due to the Pill. More likely, however, the separation is just another sign of our "disposable product" culture. Whether products or people, we use once and discard. Even our language betrays the "sex-as-product" mentality. People say they were "turned on," they "scored," or they "had sex," instead of saying they "made love."

Kathy, a 19-year-old college woman, had just made a great discovery. She shared with her counselor her newly found shortcut to lasting relationships. "I don't waste time anymore getting to know people," she said, "so I start right off by going to bed and having sex." She had yet to discover that sex without love as a "shortcut" to human intimacy can result, not only in a loss of self-respect, but also in a far worse sense of isolation and loneliness. Sex, in our culture, can be an expression of love, but not always. As social scientist Edward Ford observes in his book, *Why Marriage,* learning how to love and sustaining a warm, loving, caring relationship with another human being is a highly complicated process. Sex, as a biological function, is not nearly so complicated. "Sex only works for that one experience," comments Mr. Ford. Sex offers physical intimacy, brings two people closer together while they share the same experience, but unless there is a commitment to the love relationship, the act of sex, in itself, does not help the human relationship. Sex is the result of human intimacy, rather than the cause.[3]

Marjorie learned this painful lesson her senior year in college. Shy in manner and alone in her dorm almost every Friday and Saturday night, Marjorie had always felt a great attraction to college football players. She went to every game, filled a scrapbook with the pictures of her favorite athletes, but did not know any of the players personally. Then one Saturday night in the college tavern, she was introduced to the team's star linebacker. She had a few drinks, he dropped a few hints, and when the bar closed, they left together for his room. The next morning, over a Howard-Johnson's breakfast, she ate her toast in silence while he read the Sunday sports page. Marjorie felt let down, empty. Sex and a new kind of loneliness had come into her life at the same time.

Love can be expressed sexually, but rather than a mutual release of sexual tension or a weekend's recreation, it should be a human encounter. As Rollo May has observed:

> When we cut through all the rigmarole about roles and performance, what still remains is how amazingly important the sheer fact of intimacy of the relationship is — the meeting, the growing closeness with the excitement of not knowing where it will lead, the assertion of the self, and the giving of the self — in making a sexual encounter memorable. Is it not this intimacy that makes us return to the event in memory again and again when we need to be warmed by whatever hearths life makes available?[4]

3. Edward E. Ford, *Why Marriage* (Niles, Illinois: Argus Communications, 1974).
4. Rollo May, *Love and Will* (New York: W. W. Norton & Company, Inc., 1969), pp. 44-45.

"FALLING IN LOVE"

The second level of love is the *psychological*. Love is experienced as a pleasant sensation for which we use the word — "romance." The "icy fingers up and down your spine, the same old witchcraft when your eyes meet mine," love is understood as a spontaneous emotional reaction, an irresistible feeling. Perhaps "infatuation" is a better term, for what we are describing here is love on the emotional level. A man and a woman are attracted to each other more with the heart than with the head, and as the saying goes, they "fall in love."

Erich Fromm has described this wonderful process:

> If two people who have been strangers, as all of us are, suddenly let the wall between them break down, and feel close, feel one, this moment of oneness is one of the most exhilarating, most exciting experiences in life. It is all the more wonderful and miraculous for persons who have been shut off, isolated, without love. This miracle of sudden intimacy is often facilitated if it is combined with, or initiated by, sexual attraction and consummation.[5]

Falling in love can be a breathtaking experience, but sometimes it can also be a pitfall. So Fromm adds a caution:

> However, this type of love is by its very nature not lasting. The two persons become well acquainted, their intimacy loses more and more its miraculous character, until their antagonism, their disappointments, their mutual boredom kill whatever is left of the initial excitement. Yet, in the beginning they do not know all this: in fact, they take the intensity of the infatuation, this being "crazy" about each other,

5. Erich Fromm, *The Art of Loving* (New York: Perennial Library, Harper & Row, 1974), p. 3.

for proof of the intensity of their love, while it
may only prove the degree of their preceding
loneliness.[6]

Concerning the emotional level of love, it also needs
to be said that while love is often accompanied by feelings, sometimes there are no feelings. Too often, in
our culture, because we overemphasize the importance
of romantic love, we tend to identify all love with the
experience of pleasant sensations. This does not deny
the importance of romance, it is, however, to affirm that
deep love and caring can also exist without warm
feelings.

Perhaps a mother understands this distinction best
of all. The day a new baby is placed in her arms for the
first time, she not only loves that child, but *feels* her
love in an intense, ecstatic way. Several months later,
when her baby is teething and the mother has been up
all night, up several nights, walking the floor with her
sick child, she probably doesn't "feel" a thing. In fact,
most likely she has very negative feelings — *furious*
with her husband who never heard the baby's cry and
still sleeps; *angry* with the baby she wishes would go
back to sleep; *doubtful,* even, about marriage, and
motherhood, and most of all *guilty* about these other
feelings.

Nor is it only the sick child and an uncaring husband
that evoke such negative feelings. Teenagers can sometimes cause the same reaction. Erica, a college pro-
fessor's wife, made this discovery one morning as she
prepared breakfast:

Standing by the toaster, Erica contemplates
her children, whom she once thought the most
beautiful things on earth. Jeffrey's streaked
blond hair hangs tangled and unwashed over

6. *Ibid.,* pp. 3-4.

his eyes in front and his collar in back; he hunches awkwardly above the table, cramming fried eggs into his mouth and chewing noisily. Matilda, who is wearing a peevish expression and an orange tie-dyed jersey which looks as if it had been spat upon, is stripping the crusts off her toast with her fingers. Chomp, crunch, scratch . . .

They were a happy family once, she thinks. Jeffrey and Matilda were beautiful, healthy babies; charming toddlers; intelligent, lively, affectionate children. There are photograph albums and folders of drawings and stories and report cards to prove it. Then last year, when Jeffrey turned fourteen and Matilda twelve, they had begun to change; to grow rude, coarse, selfish, insolent, nasty, brutish and tall. It was as if she were keeping a boarding house in a bad dream, and the children she had loved were turning into awful lodgers — lodgers who paid no rent, whose leases could not be terminated. They were awful at home and abroad; in company and alone; in the morning, the afternoon and the evening.[7]

If real affection is no more than warm feelings, and genuine caring does not extend to sick babies and unappreciative adolescents, then life is fickle and true loving fleeting. Love includes something more — a decision and a deed. Since feelings flow and feelings fade, where is there a basis in emotion for a love that lasts? How can a couple promise fidelity if their love does not also include responsible choice and human commitment?

There is a difference, the difference between *affective* and *effective* love. The first refers to affectivity, emotions, the *feeling* of love; the second is concerned with the *effects* of love, its results in the real world. If it is true that "actions speak louder than words," then

7. Alison Lurie, *The War Between the Tates* (New York: Warner Paperback Library, 1975), p. 10. Copyright © 1974, Random House, Inc.

the test of true love is in its living. As an early Christian writer has said:

> I ask you, how can God's love survive in a man who has enough of this world's goods yet closes his heart to his brother when he sees him in need? . . . Let us love in deed and in truth and not merely talk about it. (1 Jn 3: 17-18)

The "deeds of love" mean more than feelings. A woman shows more real love when she walks the floor with a sick child or cooks breakfast for a hungry brood, than when she held those same children close to her heart the day they were born. That is why St. Paul, when he wrote about love in that famous section of his letter to the Christian community at Corinth, did not describe it with words of warm feelings, but in terms of deeds, of its effects:

> Love is patient; love is kind. Love is not jealous, it does not put on airs, it is not snobbish. Love is never rude, it is not self-seeking, it is not prone to anger; neither does it brood over injuries. Love does not rejoice in what is wrong but rejoices with the truth. There is no limit to love's forbearance, to its trust, its hope, its power to endure. (1 Cor 13: 4-7)

RELATIONSHIP LOVE

Spiritual — The highest meaning of love is the fully human, the mature ability "to love," to enter into an intimate, personal relationship with another human person. Lesser forms of life can mate and "have sex," they can experience sensations of pleasure and of pain, but only a human person is able to love. Unlike all other forms of life, the human spirit can know and it can choose. Only people see beneath the surface, recognize the beauty in the other, and decide in their hearts to go

out of themselves for the sake of that other and with
their lips say, "My beloved!"

St. Thomas Aquinas described love at this highest,
human level as the "ability and the desire to promote
the good of another." Erich Fromm says that "Love is
the active concern for the life and growth of that which
we love."[8] In other words, then, love in its deepest and
richest meaning is to want to live for another.

This kind of love, Jesus said, was the highest form
of human experience. He encouraged his followers to
"love one another . . . as my love has been for you, so
must your love be for each other" (Jn 13: 34). Not
content with mere words, he showed, by example, the
living of love in everyday life.

Once, when asked the meaning of love, Jesus
answered with a story. It seems, he said, there was a
traveler who had been robbed and beaten by some
hijackers. They stole his luggage, clothes and wallet,
and left the man by the side of the road, half dead. A
little later on two other travelers came along, noticed
the badly beaten man, but since both were unwilling to
become involved, they passed by without stopping.
Finally, another person came along, saw the injured man,
and stopped to help. This third traveler administered
first aid, applied simple medicines to the hijacked way-
farer's cuts and bruises, and bandaged up his wounds.
More than this, this third traveler gave the injured man a
lift to a nearby inn, put him up for the night, and paid
his bill in advance.

Jesus finished this picturesque story about the
meaning of love by saying, "Go and do the same" (Lk 10:
37). In other words, "If you want to know the meaning
of love, put yourself out for others."

Jesus' words about love are as demanding as his
stories. Once he said, "Greater love than this no man

8. *Op. cit.,* p. 22.

has, but that a man lay down his life for his friends"
(Jn 15: 13). St. John recognized the important lesson
of love in these words of Jesus when he wrote later to
an early Christian community:

> The way we came to understand love
> was that he laid down his life for us;
> we too must lay down our lives for our brothers.
> (1 Jn 3: 16)

When most of us hear love described as laying down
our lives for one another, we tend to think that those
words apply to extreme circumstances. For example,
a teenager is drowning and we swim to save his life
even at the risk of losing our own; a sudden skid on a
slippery street and a man tries to shield his pregnant
wife with his own body; the smell of smoke, the shout
of "fire!" and a mother runs through leaping flames to
save her sleeping child. These are some of the ways we
usually understand that love means laying down our lives
for our friends.

Yet when Jesus described how love's deepest meaning consists in laying down our lives for one another,
he probably meant not only the *losing* of our lives, but
the *length* of our lives. Love, in other words, means
laying down for one another what is most alive in us
now — our time, our moods, our self-interest, our feelings, ourselves. Love means we care enough to give a
little bit of our lives to those we love — everyday, in
every way.

Kevin owned a small, but rapidly expanding, delivery
service. He would leave to begin his route very early
each morning before his wife, Claire, and their three
children were awake. In the middle of the morning, on his
way back to the office, Kevin would always stop back
home for a late breakfast. Claire, while frying the eggs
and bacon, would try to talk with her husand, but Kevin,
sitting behind the paper, reading the latest basketball

scores, would usually respond with grunts. One morning, Kevin suddenly sensed his wife's loneliness, her need for adult companionship. He realized, in that moment, that love for Claire meant something as simple as laying down the paper, listening to his wife, and responding to her needs. "Let us love in deed and in truth and not merely talk about it."

Kevin began at last to put into practice the beautiful words about love that were read at the liturgy the day of his wedding to Claire:

> You begin your married life by the voluntary and complete surrender of your individual lives in the interest of that deeper and wider life which you are to have in common. Henceforth, you belong entirely to each other; you will be one in mind, one in heart and one in affection. And whatever sacrifices you may hereafter be required to make to preserve this common life, always make them generously. Sacrifice is usually difficult and irksome. Only love can make it easy; and perfect love can make it a joy. We are willing to give in proportion as we love. And when love is perfect, the sacrifice is complete. God so loved the world that he gave his only begotten Son, and the Son so loved us that he gave himself for our salvation. "Greater love than this no one has, that one lay down his life for his friends."
>
> No greater blessing can come to your married life than pure conjugal love, loyal and true to the end. May, then, this love with which you join your hands and hearts today, never fail, but grow deeper and stronger as the years go on. And if true love and the unselfish spirit of perfect sacrifice guide your every action, you can expect the greatest measure of earthly happiness that may be allotted to man in this vale of tears. The rest is in the hands of God.[9]

9. *Sanctuary Manual* (Milwaukee: The Bruce Publishing Company, 1965), p. 34-35.

Chapter 9
Love Grows By Loving

From time to time, psychologists and social workers uncover some bizarre examples of human behavior. For example, the case in New York City of the famous Collier Brothers. Two elderly, destitute men lived in a tenement where they had squirreled away for 30 years a collection of old newspapers, magazines, and trash. When the brothers died, Sanitation Department crews shoveled the ceiling-high debris out of windows into garbage trucks. At the bottom of the tons of trash they found bank books indicating accounts in the hundreds of thousands of dollars.

Then there was "Jo-Jo, the Mechanical Boy" — a disturbed teenager whose favorite plaything was a light bulb and who actually believed he was not human, but a machine. Jo-Jo fantasized that he was plugged into the nearest wall socket by an imaginary extension cord. When a visitor or nurse inadvertently stepped between the boy and the nearest wall fixture, Jo-Jo, feeling himself "unplugged," would instantly stop all activities and freeze in one position as if he were an electric train or a toy motor whose power source had been suddenly switched off.

The strangest story of all, however, is the case of the "Dwarf Children": a single woman, a waitress in a diner, had borne two children out of wedlock — a boy and a girl. Afraid of what people would say, fearful of losing her job, the single mother kept the existence of her children a secret. In her own way, the waitress was an excellent provider for her little boy and girl. She fed and clothed her children and, although she never permitted them to attend school, she taught her son and daughter the rudiments of reading and writing.

The boy and girl grew up in the back rooms of a dark apartment overlooking an enclosed courtyard where the sun never shone. Despite their strange upbringing, the children were bright, intelligent and alert. Neighbors kept hearing noises in the "empty" apartment and complained to police; the boy and girl were finally discovered by a visiting social worker. The children appeared normal in every way — with one strange exception: while the boy and girl were 13 and 14 years old, they were the size of pygmies, no larger than children of five and six. The lack of sunlight and adequate exercise had somehow stunted their normal growth.

Cases like those of the "Dwarf Children" are rarely seen by doctors and social workers. When such events do happen, they make the headlines. What psychologists and family counselors discover frequently today, however, are a kind of "dwarf people" — men and women whose emotional growth has been stunted, people who have never learned how to grow in love. A future bride or groom may be legally old enough for marriage, but if their emotional lives have never developed beyond the infantile or adolescent level, then their psychological growth will be inhibited; real warmth and caring will never happen in their marriage.

Such was the relationship between Jake and Judy. "Jake says he loves me, but he's not sure yet about marriage," Judy tearfully told her counselor. "He lived with his parents until he went away to grad school, and never paid a cent for room and board. Now that we're going together, Jake expects me to do his laundry, clean his apartment on the weekends, and type all his term papers. I don't mind helping because I really care about Jake," explained Judy, "and I know he needs me, but once in a while I wish he'd take me out to dinner or even a movie, instead of insisting we go hiking every single weekend. Jake needs me, but I wonder sometimes if he really loves me." Judy's counselor wondered, too.

Love means laying down our lives for each other, offering as a gift what is most alive in us now — our time, our personal interests, ourselves. More than mood or feelings, the proof of real love is deeds. As a radio jingle once put it: "The sounds of love don't just happen, you've got to make them!"

LOVE CAN BE LEARNED

The inability to love has been described in many ways, but most commonly as "emotional immaturity." Jake's insensitivity to Judy's needs, his self-centeredness, could have many causes: an excessive dependence upon his parents, emotional scars from the past, or the fear of rejection in the present. The fact remains, however, as psychologists and anthropologists point out, that the ability to love is a "learned response." With care and practice — and especially with the desire — people can break down the walls they have built around themselves, open their hearts to another and learn how to love.

Love *can* be learned. Dr. Richard H. Klemer carried on research over a period of 20 years with married and unmarried women in an attempt to discover the factors that make for a successful marriage relationship. In one of his studies done at a women's college, he noted that most of the new students began their social life each fall from almost the same starting point: all were away from home and very few had automobiles. But in a few months, some were dating frequently, others occasionally, while some not at all.

What made the difference? It didn't seem to be the "circumstances" (since all had relatively the same fairly restricted opportunities for dates); the difference seemed to lie in the personality factors that enabled some women to find dates and others to spend four years in college without ever having a boyfriend. As Dr. Klemer observed:

> . . . unlike either the sex ratio or the individual's physical appearance, both of which may depend upon totally uncontrollable circumstances, the ability to relate to people of the opposite sex, the ability to love and be loved, and the characteristics that make a person more marriageable *can be learned.* They can be learned or relearned or improved by almost anyone who is motivated to work at it. A person's love-ability quotient can be increased in time by study, practice, self-evaluation, and, in some cases, counselling with a professional in the field. It is not always easy, particularly if deep-seated habit patterns or emotional blocks are involved, but often a little quiet introspection and a few insights can start a person on the way.[1]

That people *can* grow and learn how to love is almost a self-evident truth, but many men and women live their lives either assuming they know all about love or expecting that love will blossom magically the day after their marriage. If they have never learned how to love, how can such people really be surprised, then, when they do not find love? Or how can they be frightened when they face a future without ever having discovered

1. Richard H. Klemer, *Marriage and Family Relationships* (New York: Harper & Row, 1970), p. 60.

love? One author, Leo F. Buscaglia, states the problem in more down-to-earth terms:

> So each man lives love in his limited fashion and does not seem to relate the resultant confusion and loneliness to this lack of knowledge about love.
>
> If he desired to know about automobiles, he would, without question, study diligently about automobiles. If his wife desired to be a gourmet cook, she'd certainly study the art of cooking, perhaps even attend a cooking class. Yet, it never seems as obvious to him that if he wants to live in love, he must spend at least as much time as the auto mechanic or the gourmet in studying love. No mechanic or cook would ever believe that by "willing" the knowledge in his field, he'd ever become an expert in it.[2]

STEPS TO LOVING

The concept of love as a "learned response" implies that it is a rational process. But it isn't — not completely. About love a certain madness prevails, a spark between two people that can never be defined or be described by statistical data. Love is "learned" in behavior appropriate to love. There are certain steps in the process of learning how to love:

1. *Love begins with loving oneself.* Real love for others has its origin in a person's own sense of worth, his self-esteem. People cannot give to another what they do not first possess themselves. This is why Jesus, when describing love, was careful to point out that it meant: ". . . to love your neighbor as yourself" (Mk 12: 33). He implied, then, that love of self comes first. Self-love means that a person feels comfortable with

2. Leo F. Buscaglia, *Love* (Thorofare, N.J.: Charles B. Slack, 1972), pp. 35-36.

himself, cares about himself and, although his plans may not always succeed, he usually behaves in such a way that afterwards he holds on to his self-respect.

Judy, in the case mentioned earlier, began to question Jake's love because of the way he used her to do his weekend cleaning and typing. Would Judy have permitted Jake to make these outrageous demands upon her free time . . . would she have acted as his cleaning lady and doormat if she had any sense of security, self-confidence and love for herself? It would seem, rather, that Judy's passive acquiescence to Jake's selfish demands was caused more by her own feelings of "worthlessness" than by any real love for Jake.

Doctor Albert Ellis, in his book *A Guide to Successful Marriage,* holds that there is a cause and effect relationship between feelings of worthlessness and mad infatuations.[3] Compulsive emotional attachments, on the part of either men or women, appear to be a way of compensating for feelings of low self-esteem. On the other hand, a person who feels good about himself, and has a sense of self-worth, will not usually tend to sudden and extreme emotional attachments.

Love *does* mean laying down our lives — what is most alive in us — for the sake of others. Love does involve drudgery, commonplace tasks like typing term papers and trips to the laundromat, but these signs of love are free gifts from one person to another, not trading stamps used to buy love. As Jesus said, describing the gift of his own life for those he loved, "No one takes it from me; I lay it down of my own free will" (Jn 10: 18).

Self-love is not self-centeredness; it is not copying the behavior of the wicked witch in *Snow White* who needed reassurance so much that she would never tire of asking her mirror, "Mirror, mirror on the wall, who's the fairest one of all?" Real self-love means that one

3. Albert Ellis, Ph.D. and Robert A. Harper, Ph.D., *A Guide to Successful Marriage* (No. Hollywood; Wilshire Book Company, 1975), pp. 96-97.

can face oneself each morning and, despite age, wrinkles, extra pounds and human failings, say, "You're the fairest of them all!" and mean it! "I may not be perfect," one says to the mirror, "but I am unique and I like myself." Loving others begins with loving oneself.

2. *Love is a process, not a product.* While love can be learned, it is not a commodity that is purchased once-and-for-all like a vacation for two to Bermuda. Cigarette advertisements, pain-reliever commercials, magazine photo-spreads — all convey the notion that somehow love just happens. Love, they pretend, requires no effort and is as easy as running through a flower-filled meadow, sharing a warm winter hearth at a ski-lodge, or walking hand-in-hand along a sunset beach.

Real love, however, is not a "package deal," is not purchased like a seven-day vacation, but is a relationship, a commitment to the unfolding, lifelong adventure of another person. It is a learning experience — a natural, evolutionary process of growth wherein a man and a woman surrender their lives to each other without terms or strings attached.

One writer, James T. Burtchaell, goes so far as to make a comparison between the process of love in a marital commitment and the call of Jesus' first followers:

> Jesus can say to a man in the crowd, "You! Follow Me" and the man has no idea where that will lead. Just so, a man can say to a woman, "Follow me, with no idea where that will lead or what I will become." And the woman in her turn says to him, "And you follow me, not knowing where I will lead you." Marriage, like Baptism, begins in faith. It is a move based simply upon trust in a person — not a policy, a religion, a moral code, a set of requirements. It is an open-ended abandonment to an unpredictable person, who is known and cherished enough that one can make the surrender.[4]

4. James T. Burtchaell, " 'Human Life' and Human Love," *Commonweal*, 15 November, 1968, pp. 245-252.

3. *Love means little things.* A photograph in a magazine or newspaper, when viewed at reading distance, appears as one picture. Closer examination with a magnifying glass, however, soon reveals that what seemed to be a single photograph actually is a composite of thousands of microscopic dots — black and gray. Many tiny units, when viewed together, make up the larger picture.

So it is with marriage. Frequently, people speak glibly of a marital relationship and say, "All you need is love." But they see only the "big picture"; they forget that married love, like a photograph, is made up of many microscopic things, many minor deeds of love. Each small act of loving represents a moment of time, a choice in a person's life, and it is these "little things" that make the whole thing possible.

Anne Roiphe, in her book, *Up the Sandbox!,* has described what these minor deeds of love comprise for a young mother who takes two small children to the park:

> The baby is struggling to move around. I put him down on my lap and take from his hand a cigarette about to go into his mouth. I watch as he crawls to the next bench, and quickly I jump up and grab him before his fingers get caught beneath a carriage wheel. I put him back in the stroller and he cries in fury. His face turns red, his period of freedom was too short, too delicious, to be given up so quickly. But I'm tired, I cannot watch him, protect him with total vigilance, and one accident a day is enough. . . . I give him a smile, I push the stroller back and forth. Elizabeth leans forward and tickles his cheek — which usually makes him laugh. Nothing works. Elizabeth pinches him too hard, the pinch ,of anger, at his tears, at his very existence. He cries louder. . . . It's early but I'm going to leave this hot playground and go to the air-conditioned pizza place on

115th Street. The children will cover themselves with tomato sauce. I will sit in the dark booth, my elbows on the shiny Formica tabletop, and play the jukebox. And then at last it will be time to go home.[5]

Love means little things. For most marriages, for most people, it means very ordinary things. The splendor of the commonplace in life — and the tragedy of so many missed opportunities — has never been expressed more poignantly than it was in the last act of Thornton Wilder's play, *Our Town.* Emily, a young wife and mother, had died; she comes back home to Grover's Corners to see herself again as she was on her 12th birthday. The vision is almost too terrible to bear:

I can't. I can't go on. Oh! Oh. It goes so fast. We don't have time to look at one another. I didn't realize. So all that was going on and we never noticed. Take me back — up the hill — to my grave. But first: Wait! One more look. Good-by, Good-by, world. Good-by, Grover's Corners . . . Mama and papa. Good-by to clocks ticking . . . and Mama's sunflowers. And food and coffee. And new-ironed dresses and hot baths . . . and sleeping and waking up. Oh, earth, you're too wonderful for anybody to realize you. Do any human beings ever realize life while they live it? — every, every minute?[6]

A REAL-LIFE EXAMPLE

4. *Love grows by loving.* The story of Therese Martin, a Frenchwoman who lived in the last century, offers a fascinating real-life example of how a person — despite many obstacles — can learn the art of loving.[7]

5. Anne Richardson Roiphe, *Up the Sandbox!* (Greenwich: Fawcett Publications, Inc., 1972), pp. 52-53. Copyright © 1970 by Anne Richardson Roiphe. Reprinted by permission of Simon & Schuster, Inc.
6. Thornton Wilder, "Our Town," *Three Plays* (New York: Harper & Brothers, 1957), p. 100. Copyright © 1938, 1957 by Thornton Wilder. By permission of publisher.
7. Ida F. Goerres, *The Hidden Face* (New York: Pantheon Books, Inc., 1959).

Therese was born in 1873 of a cultured, middle-class family. Her mother died four years later leaving Therese the youngest, and somewhat spoiled, child of a family of five daughters. Therese's middle-aged father, while loving her tenderly, was inclined to be withdrawn and moody; he eventually suffered a complete mental breakdown. After a fairly sheltered childhood, and a period of headaches and nervous hysteria apparently related to the death of her mother, Therese felt she had a religious vocation. She entered a cloistered convent at the incredibly young age of 15. While her adolescent dreams of a religious vocation were very romantic and idealistic, Therese soon learned that the day-to-day reality of life in this convent was entirely different. The young woman had expected the long fasts, straw mattresses, and unheated rooms, but nothing in her experience had prepared her for the narrow-minded and limited people who lived behind those convent walls. Therese had hoped to find friendship and love; she discovered, instead, that the convent contained an atmosphere of petty jealousies, constant bickerings, and very little love. Many of the problems were due to the influence of the emotionally unstable Mother Superior who treated her cat with more tenderness and compassion than she showed the sisters who belonged to the religious community.[8]

Therese Martin's reaction to these strange people and this extremely unusual situation was simple and direct — she decided to love them, especially one of the nuns who was old and arthritic. Three times each day, Therese escorted this crippled sister from chapel to the convent dining room. The old woman was impossible to please; if Therese held on too tightly, the sister would scream that Therese was trying to pull her over; if Therese didn't hold on tightly enough, then the old

8. *Ibid.,* pp. 200-201.

woman complained that she was going to fall! So, unable to please the chronic complainer either way, Therese would somehow guide the old nun into the dining room, sit her at the table, fold back her sleeves, and cut her bread into little pieces. Last of all, she would place a fork in the senior sister's crippled hand; then, said Therese, "I gave her, before I left, my very best smile."[9]

Another of the nuns, by her dull personality and know-it-all attitude, "managed to irritate me in everything she did," explained Therese. But during the rare recreation periods, Therese would go out of her way to sit with this difficult person and attempt to carry on a normal, friendly conversation. Therese showed the obnoxious nun so much attention, as a matter of fact, that her own blood sisters, who were also nuns in the convent, grew jealous and complained that Therese was neglecting them.

In 1897, at the age of 24, Therese Martin died of tuberculosis. Before her death, she confided to one of her natural sisters, Celine, that the most difficult aspect of her life in the convent had not been the cold winter nights and long Lenten fasts, but the tedious nun whose personality had been so irritating. "I was stunned," Celine later related. "I had always thought this sister was her best friend."

What was Therese's secret? How had she been able not only to tolerate this unattractive person, but also actually learn to love her? Therese's answer was as uncomplicated as it was uncompromising: "I made up my mind to treat her as if I loved her best of all."[10]

Therese Martin had made a very simple decision. She chose to give as a gift to this dull sister the only thing she could really call her own in that French con-

9. Ronald Knox, trans., *Autobiography of a Saint* (London: Harvill Press, Ltd., 1958), pp. 296-297.
10. Goerres, *op. cit.,* pp. 243-244.

vent — her free time and her full attention. She *practiced* the "art of loving" and in this way she learned how to love.

It is interesting to read how the insights of a great psychologist, the late Abraham H. Maslow, tend to confirm the lesson of love discovered so many years ago by St. Therese of Lisieux, as Therese Martin is now known. For Maslow writes:

> Let us think of life as a process of choices, one after another. At each point, there is a progression choice and a regression choice. There may be a movement toward defense, toward safety, toward being afraid, but over on the other side, there is the growth choice. To make the growth choice, instead of the fear choice, a dozen times a day is to move a dozen times a day toward self-actualization.[11]

MARRIAGE A SCHOOL OF LOVE

Marriage in modern America may appear rather remote from a 19th-century French convent, but the opportunities offered are the same — to make the growth choice or the fear choice, to grow in love or to refuse to love. Whether in convent or in kitchen, romantic love is soon over; unrealistic expectations begin to fade in the cold light of reality. It is at that precise moment, as it is in any vocation, that the choice is offered. On the one hand, with the ease by which the words are used today, a couple can say that they are incompatible, unfulfilled, that they acted in haste, that the person they married is different or that they are no longer in love — this is one choice. On the other hand, the choice offered is to say "yes" to the words spoken so easily on the day of marriage and to begin to love, to lay down what is most alive for the sake of the other. It is a free

11. Cited by Herbert Fensterheim and Jean Baer, *Don't Say Yes When You Want to Say No* (New York: Dell Publishing Co., Inc. 1975), p. 58.

human choice — to offer love or to withhold it.

A husband comes home at evening after a long, hard day in the office jungle. He feels, some days, that he is a failure, that he's beating his head against the wall and getting nowhere in his career. This man, the moment he walks in the kitchen door at day's end to meet the woman of his life, is offered a very simple choice. He can greet his wife with a grunt, retreat into his feelings of self-pity, put up a wall of silence, and hide behind the evening paper — that is the regression choice. The same moment also offers a growth choice, an opportunity to love. As he walks in the kitchen door, the husband can choose to lay down, at that instance, what is most alive to him, what problems are most pressing — his fatigue, his failures, his feelings of self-pity — and he can choose to respond to the human being that waits to greet him. Aware of her presence, attentive to her needs, he can lay down the unopened paper, put his arm around her waist and suggest, "Why don't you go out and sit on the porch, while I finish getting supper?"

It is also a woman's choice. The sink is plugged, the car won't start, one of the children has a temperature of 103 degrees; the wife has not been out of the house all day, is feeling trapped, and is just a little lonely. She, too, is offered a regression choice or a growth choice. She can complain about her day, wonder out loud why her husband was late in coming home, demand that he take a plunger to the sink, hide behind her own wall of silence. These responses would reflect her regression choice. On the other hand, she can choose to grow. She can lay down, for his sake, the feelings that are most alive in her at that moment — her fears, frustrations, loneliness — and respond to his needs. So she turns down the stove, greets him with a kiss and then asks with a smile, "How was your day?" She can then suggest they eat together later, after the children have been fed and he has had time to read the evening paper.

A simple scenario without a fixed final scene. There are many faces of love, many opportunities to choose. Each husband and each wife write a personal ending to that script and a thousand similar ones every day of their lives. Ultimately, the success of a marriage entails many steps, and each step represents a choice. As Therese Martin said, "I made up my mind to treat her as if I loved her best of all."

There is a story told about a Marine sergeant named Jimmy Mahoney. He was married shortly before going overseas in World War II, but he and his bride had never had the chance to celebrate a Christmas together. He came back from the Pacific in December of 1945, hoping against hope that he'd make it home in time enough, not only to be with his young wife for Christmas, but also with enough time to buy her a special present. Flights had been canceled; planes had been grounded, but finally he flew into New York City late on Christmas Eve, after all the stores were closed.

He took a cab from the airport, but noticed on his way into the Bronx that a drugstore was still open. He stopped the cab and made a purchase. Then, finally home, he rang the doorbell of his little apartment. When his bride opened the door, late that Christmas Eve, she gasped. He was wrapped like a gift package — with a great big red ribbon and a bow across his chest and a card which read, "To Mary from Jimmy, with all my love." They laughed and cried as they fell into each other's arms, because they both knew that he had given her, for their first Christmas, the one gift she had wanted most of all — himself.

Chapter 10
Friends and Lovers

The Prince was especially relieved as he came home to his castle that night. To begin with, he had experienced a difficult time dispatching a particularly ferocious, fire-breathing dragon. Then some of the younger knights had questioned his swordsmanship, suggesting that there were easier ways to do in a beast. They had even hinted that the Prince was losing his touch. So it was nice to gallop across the moat on his white charger, pull up the drawbridge, and bar the great oaken doors. Home was his castle, the Prince mused, and here, at least, he was king — Master of all his domain.

So he was stunned when the Princess, after greeting him with a kiss, made a surprising announcement: "Guess what! I've got a job . . . take off your suit of armor and I'll tell you all about it!" "A job?" roared the Prince. "What about your castle in the clouds — straightening its many rooms, cleaning its many corridors, and feeding its many guests? Besides, who'd employ a Princess?" "That's exactly it," answered the Princess, "I've been hired as a professional guide for *Castle Tours Limited!*"

"Fix me a drink," gasped the Prince as he col-
lapsed onto his throne. "Fix it yourself," re-
torted the Princess, "I'm off to work — and
don't forget to give your many sons their supper!"

Contemporary marriage is in a process of change —
its definitions, its roles, its expectations. No longer
does marriage offer as many of the "essential services,"
functions like survival, identity and education, in quite
the same way as before. So the question is not one of
changing marital roles and functions, but, rather, the
significance of that change. Is it growth or decline?
Will marriage as an institution survive, or will it cease
to be a valid, human experience?

Many people today sincerely believe that marriage
as an institution has failed. The outspoken guests on
the Johnny Carson and Merv Griffin talk shows, the
angry words of lesbian feminists, even a *New York Times*
magazine article which captions marriage as a "long
inhibiting tradition" — all these do not so much attack
the concept of traditional marriage as they attempt to
make sense out of it and redefine it for themselves.
Many alternatives to marriage are suggested; three of
the most widely publicized are: couples living together
without benefit of a formal ceremony; group marriages
where sexually free couples swap mates; and the
"swinging-singles," no-strings-attached life-style.

SERIOUS CHALLENGE?

These contemporary phenomena raise a whole new
set of questions about the meaning of marriage. Are
they passing fads or life-styles of the future? How
seriously do these alternatives challenge traditional
marriage? The answers require a closer examination:
1. *Living Together Before Marriage.* As an increasing number of parents are discovering to their dismay,

more couples than ever before seem to be settling down to "play house" today without benefit of wedding ring or formal ceremony. Census Bureau figures bear out these parental misgivings. Between 1960 and 1970, when the number of married couples increased by 10 percent, the number of unmarried couples living together grew by 820 percent. Other, less formal, hints of a boom in these live-in arrangements are the look of domesticity in couples shopping together for staple food items on Friday nights or late Sunday mornings in near-campus foodliners and supermarkets; the growing number of couples who "use the same address" when registering for a Newman Center premarriage course; the former student who calls his college chaplain long distance with a request to officiate at his wedding and then adds a quiet clarification, "You understand, Father, that Judy and I already consider ourselves married."

Couples living together before marriage has been described by one writer as an "uncertain togetherness,"[1] for the phenomenon seems to be less a sign of liberation from traditional marriage than it is an indication of uncertainty and fear of failure. While some live-in arrangements are terribly dehumanizing experiences, others may be a way by which couples, caught between apparently conflicting needs for identity and intimacy, buy themselves time to acquire "space" for their relationship to grow into a secure and lasting commitment to each other. Human motivation is complex, not easily analyzed, but behind the hesitancy of some couples to affirm their commitment with a public religious ceremony, there lies an awareness of the seriousness and sacredness of the marital contract that other couples, who skip to the altar so blithely and mouth sacred vows so glibly, scarcely sense at all.

Couples who choose to live together before mar-

---

1. J. Murray Elwood, "Uncertain Togetherness" *Marriage and Family Living,* August, 1975, pp. 23-26.

riage are not romantic figures, for, at best, such a relationship *is* an "uncertain togetherness" with no predictability for the future, no promise of fidelity. But the fact that such "arrangements" do happen more frequently today says more about the insecurities of the age than it does about the religious and ethical infidelities of the couples involved.

2. *Group Marriage.* Robert Rimmer's novels, *The Harrad Experiment* and *Proposition 31,* have described the group experiments of sexual swingers and swappers. His books are avidly read and, occasionally, seriously discussed in university "Alternatives to Marriage" courses. The books remain, however, more fiction than fact. Unlike the dramatic increase of couples living together before marriage, the comparable evidence of couples grouping together after marriage is scant.

One attempt to describe "multilateral marriages" was the book *Group Marriage* by Larry and Joan Constantine.[2] Their study, however, involved only 33 such marriages with in-depth analysis of 11 group relationships. Another writer, doing research on the subject, heard a speaker at a meeting of family sociologists say that group marriage was "wonderful for children" and that it also, of course, "helps adults grow." "Group marriage may not supplant traditional marriage in five or ten years," said the speaker, "but it is on the way." When the reporter then asked what evidence supported such a claim, the lecturer replied that he had observed three such cases of mate-swapping and had heard of 12 others.[3]

Viewed from the perspective of 93 million married Americans, group marriage thus appears as a tiny drop in an ocean of monogamy. As one reviewer described it, after reading the Constantine book:

2. Larry L. and Joan M. Constantine, *Group Marriage: A Study of Contemporary Multilateral Marriage* (New York: The Macmillan Company, 1973).
3. Lester Velie, "The Myth of the Vanishing Family," *Reader's Digest,* February, 1973, pp. 114-115.

My own impression is that group marriages are fleeting, fragile, faddish and ephemeral experiences, indulged in by the far-out few. They are part of the mood of rampant experimentation, confusion, disenchantment and permissiveness which has gripped the spirit of our times. If I were to venture a prediction, it would be that this groping, aimless period of trial and error will soon have spent itself. There will come a time when terms like "fidelity" will not be regarded as four-letter words.[4]

3. *Swinging Singles.* Census studies estimate that the number of single people — unmarried, divorced and widowed — is growing in our society. Of the 40 million singles in 1975 and the 46 million estimated in 1980, half are between the ages of 18 and 29.[5] This is the group sometimes described — or characterized — as the "swinging singles." Glamorized by *Playboy* and glorified in such books as *Beyond Monogamy* as belonging to a "liberating life-style," young adult singles comprise a unique subculture with their own social patterns, interests, and needs. Singles clubs of all kinds are becoming increasingly popular — especially in tennis, travel, and skiing — but the most persistent symbol of the young adult life-style remains the dark and anonymous singles bar, which is popular because of the social and sexual pressures that force some men and women into a desperate "open market" search for companionship.

The single male predicament has been described in George Gilder's *Naked Nomads,*[6] which paints an alarming statistical portrait of the single man: he earns far less than the married man; he is roughly twice as likely to commit crimes, to go to jail, and to die early; he is

4. Robert Lee, rev. of "Group Marriage," by Larry L. and Joan M. Constantine. Copyright © 1973 Christian Century Foundation. Reprinted by permission from May 30, 1973 issue of *The Christian Century,* p. 632.
5. "Rise of the 'Singles' — 40 Million Free Spenders," *U.S. News & World Report,* Oct. 7, 1974, p. 54.
6. George Gilder, *Naked Nomads* (New York: Quadrangle, 1974).

also much more likely to develop physical and emotional illness and commit suicide.[7] While recognizing that he draws this negative image in broad, sweeping generalizations, Gilder still feels that the life of the bachelor is marked by an inability to sustain a commitment and by a lack of orientation toward the future. The single male, at least as George Gilder pictures him, tends to drift from city to city, from job to job, from bed to bed.

Looking for Mr. Goodbar,[8] Judith Rossner's popular novel, depicts the life of a single woman, Theresa Dunn, who by day is a dedicated teacher in a ghetto school but at night cruises New York's singles bars, arriving alone, but usually leaving with a pickup. The final scene of Theresa's life is her brutal murder by the last of her many one-night stands. She is the victim of a vicious killer, but she has also victimized the many men in her life by her teasings, put-downs, games-playing and, especially, by taunting the one man who really cared about her with details of her casual relationships. *Looking for Mr. Goodbar* describes the New York singles bar scene and tries to recreate fictionally the dark side of the lives of some single women, depicting with frightening realism their insecurities, their mating games, their lonely, desperate search among the naked nomads for "Mr. Wonderful."

All singles are not, of course, unstable, uncommitted or sexually promiscuous, but the difficulty some find in making a commitment or in saying "I love you," unmasks the myth of the "swinging single" life-style as an honest alternative to marriage. The "language of liberation" heard on the singles bar scene — "it doesn't make sense to get too committed when you're always growing and changing," "I'm not ready to get tied down at this stage of my life," "I have to be free to grow and I want you

7. George Gilder, "In Defense of Monogamy," *Commentary,* November, 1974, pp. 31-36.
8. Judith Rossner, *Looking for Mr. Goodbar* (New York: Simon and Schuster, 1975).

to be free, too" — hints at a more basic lack of a sense of identity. As psychologist William Kilpatrick has observed in his book, *Identity and Intimacy,*[9] the ability to make a commitment, to love, depends upon a more fundamental sense of identity. Identity backs up love the way gold stands behind federal reserve notes. Without identity, commitments are halfhearted, we drift aimlessly, unable to trust, fearful that what little sense of self we possess may be drowned in the depths of an intimate relationship with another.

The critics of marriage and the family are very outspoken, but reappraisals of the basic institutions in society are nothing new; they seem to occur at transitional periods in human history. The alternatives to marriage suggested by such social commentators, however, seem to create more problems than they cure.

CHANGING ROLE

Dr. Salvador Minuchin of the Philadelphia Child Guidance Clinic has pointed out that the family and the institution of marriage are not deteriorating, but merely undergoing a normal process of adjustment to the changes in society, just as they have adjusted in the past. "There is nothing else to replace it (the family) as an emotional center of people's lives, or as the transmitter of culture or for raising children," says Dr. Minuchin.[10]

The changing, evolving role of marriage in society might be compared to a physician's role in a community. When the young doctor first opens his office he is a general practitioner — checking blood pressures, setting broken bones, writing prescriptions for everyday ailments. After a few years as a family physician, he goes away for study, and new clinical experience, then returns to his community as a specialist, perhaps a skilled

9. William Kilpatrick, Ph.D., *Identity and Intimacy* (New York: Dell Publishing Co., 1975), pp. 1-2.
10. "Interview on the Family," *U.S. News and World Report,* January 13, 1975, p. 44.

neurosurgeon. He no longer provides the ordinary services such as routine blood pressures and general physical examinations. His surgical skills are now more specialized, but much more valuable to his community.

So it is with marriage. As suggested earlier, marriage no longer plays the same kind of role in people's lives as it once did. But the fact that these former "services" are no longer provided — functions such as survival, education, and extended family — does not mean that marriage as an institution has failed. Marriage *is* performing fewer functions than in earlier days, but the satisfactions it still offers are more specialized and much more critically important than ever before in the lives of married couples.

Marriage will continue to play a significant part in the lives of most men and women because:

1. *Marriage provides a support structure* enabling people to preserve their basic humanity. Just as certain New England towns have continued customs and traditions from the days of the American revolution into the present, so marriage is a "carrier" or a vehicle of *trust*.

In sports, the athlete is only as good as last season's record; in the arts, the writer is only as renowned as his last book; in academe, the student only as successful as last semester's index; but marriage, ideally, does away with the need for persons to be always starting over at an emotional "ground zero," wasting time and psychic energy proving themselves to each other over and over again. Public promises before families and friends make it possible for two human beings to count on certain things.

2. *Marriage preserves an experience of intimacy.* As society becomes more mechanized and impersonal, with fewer opportunities for primary group contacts, and as institutions and organizations become more computerized and technological, marriage can emerge as an even more critically important source of warmth, loving care and affectivity than ever before. Marriage is

the place where human beings can reach out and touch each other, psychically as well as physically.

Frequently today, engaged couples will describe their relationship by saying, "We're best friends besides being lovers." For most of them, this is the role marriage will play in their lives, for in America married men and women have each other as friends to a degree unusual in the rest of the world. At other times and in other cultures, men sought companionship and emotional warmth at the local pub or with their paramour. Today marriage has become an island of human warmth for two in the cold sea of impersonalization.

3. *Marriage offers meaning to adults* and surrounds children with the caring atmosphere they need to acquire their own values in life. In a culture with many conflicting value systems, it is critically important for a sense of self-worth and the preservation of one's own ideals, that each person have the emotional support, acceptance and care of significant others who understand and share these same values. In the day-to-day struggle to make sense out of life, marriage is the one place where most people find support for their values, healing for their wounds, someone who will say, "It's all right, I understand."

When Brian and Andrea stood before the altar 12 long years ago and surrendered their lives into each other's hands, those of us present for their wedding heard their words and were deeply moved. But like children in a First Communion class who recite by rote the promise to "love God with my whole heart," the bride and groom spoke words that day they hardly knew the meaning of: "for richer, for poorer, in sickness and in health, until death do us part."

Their parents in the front pews had a good idea what those words meant. The priest at the altar also had some understanding. Now Andrea and Brian, too, these many years later, have come to learn that growing together, like learning how to love, is a slow, painful process — a moving beyond personal needs and away from human selfishness out to each other, out to others.

Marriage is not the promised land, the end of all life's worries and cares; nor is human love a romantic rainbow. Rather, it is a slow process of growth with another fragile person. Nevertheless, society has yet to suggest as supportive an alternative as marriage for intimate, human relationships. Perhaps it never will.

T. S. Eliot said it best of all in his play, *The Cocktail Party*. A woman, Celia, has gone to her psychiatrist, seeking help with her marriage. The therapist suggests that for happiness in marriage a couple must avoid "excessive expectation," learn to give and take in the usual ways, and finally grow tolerant of themselves and others. "Is that the best life?" Celia asks. The psychiatrist replies:

> It is a good life. Though you will not know
> how good
> Till you come to the end. But you will want
> nothing else,
> And the other life will be only like a book
> You have read once, and lost. In a world
> of lunacy,
> Violence, stupidity, greed . . . it is a good life.[11]

---

11. T. S. Eliot, *The Cocktail Party,* in *The Complete Poems and Plays, 1909-1950* (New York: Harcourt, Brace, Jovanovich, Inc., 1952), p. 364.